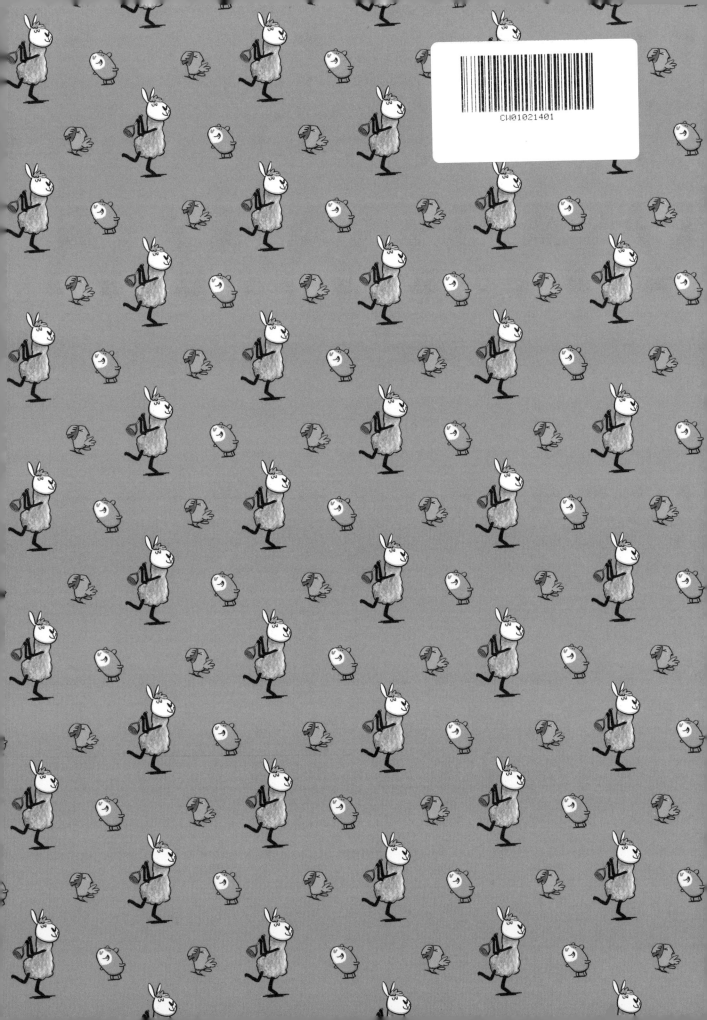

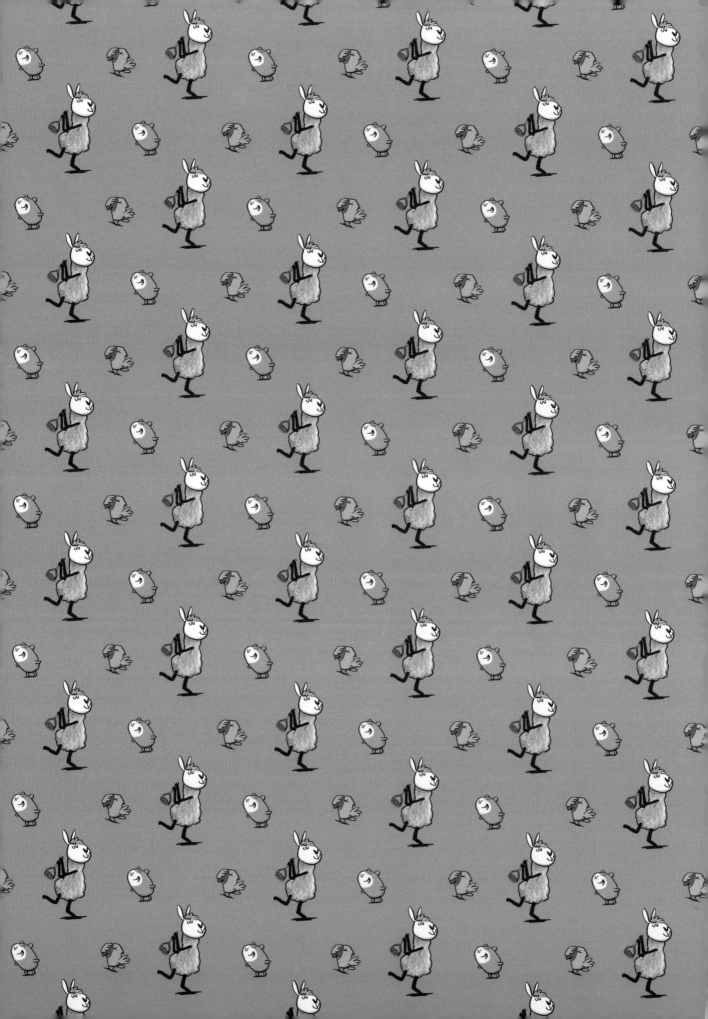

LLAMA can't COOK

But YOU can!

Noodle Juice Ltd
www.noodle-juice.com
Stonesfield House, Stanwell Lane,
Great Bourton, Oxfordshire, OX17 1QS

First published in Great Britain 2023
Copyright © Noodle Juice Ltd 2023

Written by Sarah Walden 2022
Illustrations by Mr Griff 2022
Photography by Tina Knowles

ISBN: 978-1-915613-22-6
3 5 7 9 10 8 6 4 2

Llama Can't Cook, But You Can!

CONTENTS

Let's get cooking!

Welcome!

This very different cookery book teaches you how to use key ingredients and flavours, and how to create delicious food for your family and friends. By the end of this book, you – and hopefully Llama – will be able to cook over 70 fantastic dishes from around the world.

Each chapter deals with either a key ingredient or a core skill. At every stage, our cast of friendly animals will be advising you (or not!) on how to make the most delicious food you can!

There are also handy cooking tips and techniques (see pages 108–111), as well as fascinating facts about the ingredients used in the recipes, and the origins of some of your favourite meals.

> Each recipe will have step-by-step instructions and photos to show you exactly what you should be doing!

Meet the team

GUINEA PIG

The expert chef. Guinea Pig has plenty of advice to help you cook the best food you can.

PARROT

In charge of Health and Safety, Parrot will remind you to be careful when using sharp knives, the hob or the oven. If he says you should ask a grown-up to help, then make sure you do!

LLAMA

Has a lot to learn!

> Slow and steady wins the race!

GROWN-UP'S HELP NEEDED!

> But I can cook, really I can! I just need a bit more practice.

4

Food allergies

Some people have food allergies or intolerances. Recipes that contain dairy, eggs, gluten, nuts, shellfish or wheat are clearly marked, and state where those ingredients are optional. There are plenty of delicious vegetarian recipes too.

We don't often need storage containers around here!

Food storage

You may need to store what you've cooked – so make sure you have plastic storage containers to hand to keep your delicious food fresh.

I wonder why?

Essential Equipment

Every recipe in this book can be made with the utensils shown here and a little bit of manual dexterity!

You will also need a liquidiser – handheld or stand version – and a mini food processor.

That means your hands!

Not sure how dexterous I shall be!

large flat casserole

baking tray

mixing bowl

tea towel

oven gloves

baking parchment

fork

sharp knife

scissors

juicer

colander

plastic bag

soufflé dish

grater

wooden spoon

spatula

sieve

masher

It's a good idea to wear an apron to keep your clothes clean while cooking.

I think this could get messy!

Be careful when using sharp knives or graters and always make sure a grown-up is supervising.

Using a microwave

Always make sure you have a grown-up present, and never ever put anything metal into the microwave. Remember to always use oven gloves when getting food in and out too.

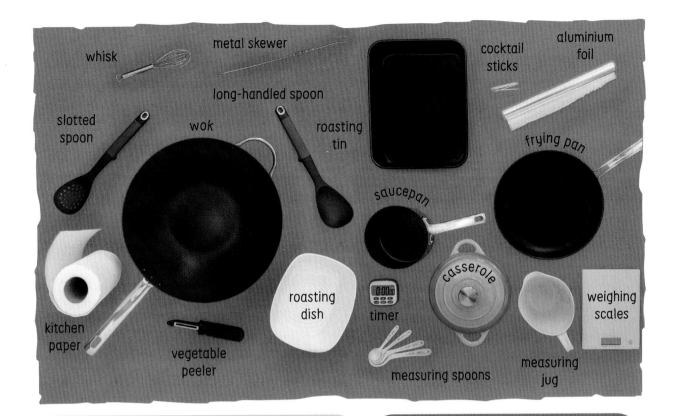

whisk

metal skewer

cocktail sticks

aluminium foil

long-handled spoon

slotted spoon

wok

roasting tin

frying pan

saucepan

casserole

roasting dish

timer

weighing scales

kitchen paper

vegetable peeler

measuring spoons

measuring jug

Oven

A lot of the recipes use an oven. Different ovens can cook at different temperatures so some recipes might need a bit longer in the oven than the recipe suggests, or a bit less. The Celsius temperatures listed in the book are for an oven with a fan, so if you aren't using a fan oven, please increase the temperature by 20°C.

Non-stick pans or trays

Lots of pans and trays have a non-stick coating. This is great as it means that food doesn't stick to them, so they are easy to clean. However, you shouldn't use metal utensils in non-stick pans or trays, as they can damage the coating. Use wooden or plastic ones instead.

I think this fish pie needed a bit less time in the oven!

We'll also be using the grill – this can get very hot and cook your dishes very quickly, so always keep an eye on whatever is under the grill!

Don't leave the kitchen if you have your grill on and definitely don't forget to wear your oven gloves!

Essential Ingredients

Here are most of the ingredients you will need to make the recipes in the book. There are lots of different types of pasta and rice, as well as spices and herbs. Why not experiment with flavours you like?

I thought spaghetti grew on trees!

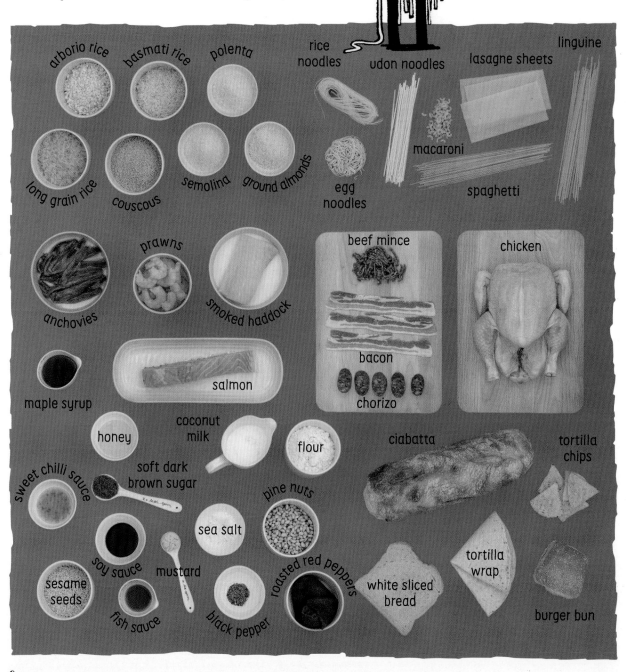

arborio rice · basmati rice · polenta · rice noodles · udon noodles · lasagne sheets · linguine · macaroni · long grain rice · couscous · semolina · ground almonds · egg noodles · spaghetti · prawns · beef mince · chicken · anchovies · smoked haddock · bacon · chorizo · maple syrup · salmon · honey · coconut milk · flour · ciabatta · tortilla chips · sweet chilli sauce · soft dark brown sugar · pine nuts · sea salt · tortilla wrap · sesame seeds · soy sauce · mustard · roasted red peppers · white sliced bread · fish sauce · black pepper · burger bun

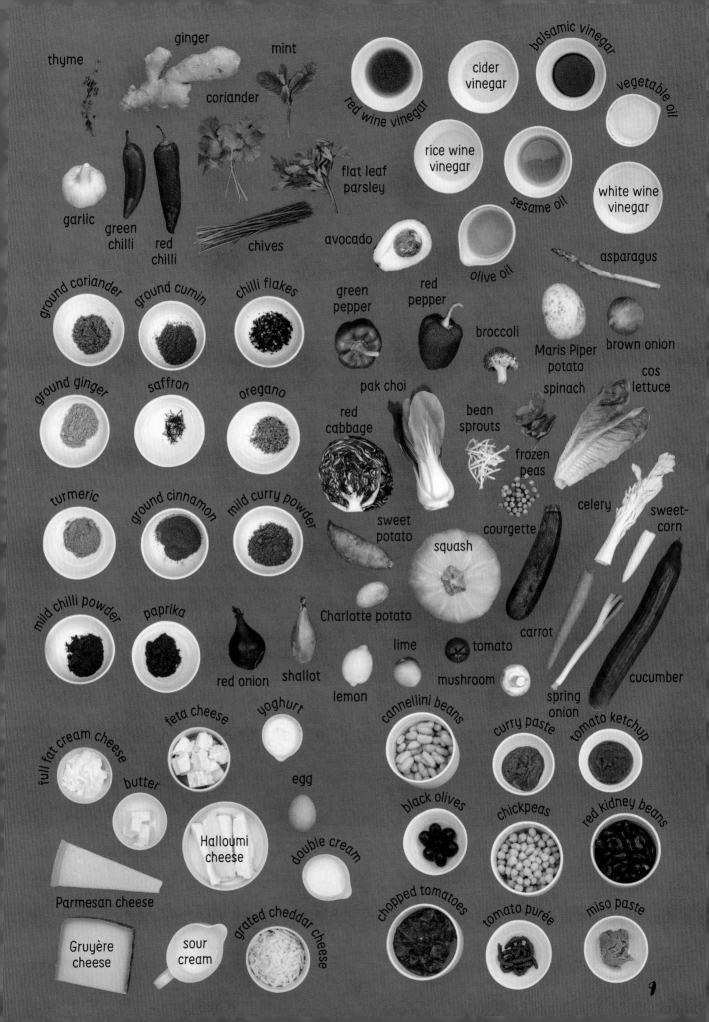

thyme

ginger

mint

coriander

garlic

green chilli

red chilli

flat leaf parsley

chives

avocado

red wine vinegar

cider vinegar

balsamic vinegar

vegetable oil

rice wine vinegar

sesame oil

white wine vinegar

olive oil

asparagus

ground coriander

ground cumin

chilli flakes

green pepper

red pepper

broccoli

Maris Piper potato

brown onion

ground ginger

saffron

oregano

pak choi

spinach

cos lettuce

red cabbage

bean sprouts

frozen peas

turmeric

ground cinnamon

mild curry powder

sweet potato

courgette

celery

sweet-corn

squash

mild chilli powder

paprika

Charlotte potato

lime

tomato

carrot

red onion

shallot

lemon

mushroom

cucumber

spring onion

full fat cream cheese

feta cheese

yoghurt

cannellini beans

curry paste

tomato ketchup

butter

egg

black olives

chickpeas

red kidney beans

Halloumi cheese

double cream

Parmesan cheese

chopped tomatoes

tomato purée

miso paste

Gruyère cheese

sour cream

grated cheddar cheese

Getting Started

Cooking is thought to be more of an art than a science, which often means that you can be flexible with the ingredients you use.

I don't think we like lemon that much!

If you like the flavour of lemon in your fish pie, then add a little more than the recipe says. If you really don't like parsley, then don't include it in your dish.

However, each of the recipes in this book has been tested to make sure that it works, so practise these first before you start to experiment with different flavour combinations!

Weighing and measuring

Another good idea is to practise using your weighing scales. Scales are really important as they help you make sure that you have the right amount of each ingredient. Most electronic scales let you set the weight to zero once you have put your measuring bowl on them, so you only weigh the amount you need without having to do any complicated maths!

Follow the recipe

When you start to cook, read the recipe carefully first to make sure you understand what you need to do. Assemble all the ingredients and equipment before you begin so that you have everything you need.

Stock

Some recipes use stock to add flavour. You can buy stock in many different forms – you can even make it yourself! Fresh, cubes or concentrate all work in these recipes.

Eggs

All recipes have been made using medium-sized eggs.

Washing your hands

This is very important – you must keep your hands clean when cooking, especially if you are handling raw meat.

We use chicken, beef, fish and vegetable stock in our recipes!

Make sure you wash your hands after touching raw meat or fish, so you don't contaminate any other ingredients!

Cooking on the hob

When you use the hob, you can cook food in lots of different ways. Here are the most common methods:

Boil. Food, usually vegetables, is cooked in boiling water – very hot water with lots of big bubbles.

Simmer. Food is cooked in water, but the water is not as hot as boiling, with small bubbles that don't break the surface.

Steam. Good for vegetables or fish, food is cooked in a steamer with a lid above simmering water.

Brown. Food, often meat, is cooked over a high heat in order to turn it brown – or caramelised.

Fry or sauté. This method cooks food in a very small amount of oil in a frying pan, over medium to high heat.

Stir-fry. Often in a wok, using a high heat, you quickly cook small pieces of food, stirring all the time.

Stew. Normally a slow gentle method of cooking, you stew food in a covered container with liquid over a low heat.

Be very careful if you have boiling liquid in a pan!

Washing fruit and vegetables

Before using fruit or vegetables, make sure that you have washed them thoroughly first and then dried them off. Mushrooms really don't like water, so it's better to brush or wipe off any dirt and then peel them.

If you have to peel the vegetable or fruit before using it, such as an onion or a banana, you don't need to wash it!

Seasoning

Seasoning means to add flavour to food. Normally this is salt and pepper. If you oversalt something it won't taste very nice, so add small amounts at a time, and always taste what you're cooking!

KEY INGREDIENT
#1 Eggs

Eggs are really versatile and can be used in many different recipes. The humble egg is brilliant for breakfast, or a quick lunch, and is really good for you too. Here are six tasty ways to cook an egg.

Fun Facts

Eggs contain lots of protein as well as 18 different vitamins and minerals.

Fresh eggs sink in water and rotten eggs float to the top.

Eggs consist of an egg shell, a yellow yolk and an egg white, which surrounds the yolk.

But I like floating!

You shouldn't eat the egg shell!

Ingredients

Eggs – see each recipe for the number you need

Slices of bread – see each recipe for the number you need

Butter, for spreading and for scrambling

1 teaspoon white wine vinegar, for poaching

1 tablespoon vegetable oil per egg, for frying

3 tablespoons milk or cream, for scrambling

Salt and pepper

You will need a saucepan, a frying pan, kitchen paper, a saucer and egg cups.

ALLERGIES

Dairy, eggs, gluten, wheat

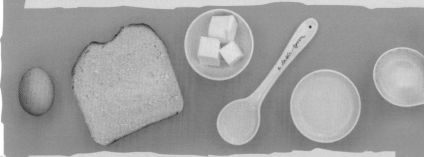

VEGETARIAN

Soft or Hard-boiled Eggs

Soft or hard-boiled eggs are cooked in a pan of boiling water. The longer the egg cooks, the more solid the yolk will become. Hard-boiled eggs are good for salads or sandwich fillings. Soft-boiled eggs are delicious with toast soldiers!

NUMBER OF SERVINGS 2

TIMINGS 10 MINUTES

I'm not sure I would like to dip a soldier in my egg.

They're made from toast, silly!

Method

1 You will need two eggs. Half fill your saucepan with water and bring to the boil. Slowly lower the eggs into the water using a long-handled spoon.

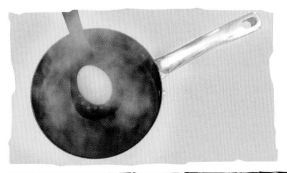

2 For a runny yolk, set your timer for 4–5 minutes. For a hard-boiled egg, set your timer for 8–9 minutes.

3 If making toast soldiers, toast two slices of bread. Once toasted, allow to cool slightly before spreading with butter and cutting into strips.

4 When the timer goes off, remove the pan from the heat and carefully lift out the eggs with a slotted spoon. For hard-boiled eggs, immediately place the eggs in a bowl of cold water to stop them cooking any further.

5 When you need the hard-boiled eggs, gently roll the eggs on a hard surface to crack the shell. Peel off the shell and membrane.

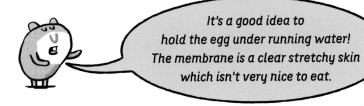

It's a good idea to hold the egg under running water! The membrane is a clear stretchy skin which isn't very nice to eat.

6 For runny eggs and soldiers, place the egg into an egg cup and carefully cut the top off, about 1cm from the pointy end of the egg. Serve with toast soldiers for dipping.

Be careful as the eggs will be hot.

Fried Eggs

Fried eggs are cooked in a frying pan using a little oil and are perfect for cooked breakfasts or fried egg sandwiches. They can be served 'sunny side up' with the yolk facing up or 'over easy', which means flipped so the egg white is on top.

The trick to keeping a runny yolk is to make sure that the frying pan isn't too hot and to take your time.

Be careful with hot fat as it can spit!

Llamas spit really well when we're angry!

NUMBER OF 2 SERVINGS

TIMINGS 5 MINUTES

Method

1 You will need two fresh eggs. Crack the eggs onto a saucer to make each one easier to add to the pan.

2 Heat a tablespoon of vegetable oil on a medium heat. Slide the egg into the pan. Repeat with the other egg.

3 Cover with a lid and cook for 3 minutes on a low heat. If you would like your eggs over easy, use a spatula to flip them over 30 seconds before the time is up. Season and serve.

Poached Eggs

Poaching means to cook gently in water. This can be tricky, but if you follow these simple steps, you'll be making perfect poached eggs every time.

NUMBER OF 1 SERVINGS

TIMINGS 10 MINUTES

Method

1 You will need one very fresh egg. Crack your egg onto a saucer to make it easier to add to the pan.

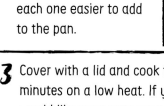

2 Pour some water into your pan – at least 5cm deep – and bring to the boil. Then turn the heat down slightly, so the water is simmering. Add a teaspoon of white wine vinegar to the pan.

3 Swirl the water in the pan to create a whirlpool.

I should still float though!

4 Slowly slide the egg into the pan and cook for 3–4 minutes to make sure the egg white is completely set. Make your toast.

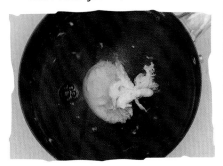

5 To remove the egg from the pan, use a slotted spoon and drain the egg on kitchen paper. Serve on a slice of buttered toast.

Scrambled Eggs

Once you know how to scramble eggs, you'll always be able to make a delicious breakfast or supper dish. You can add all sorts of other ingredients to them too.

NUMBER OF **2** SERVINGS

TIMINGS 5–8 MINUTES

Like this, you mean?

The trick is to make sure you don't overcook the eggs – otherwise they might bounce like rubber!

Method

1 Crack two eggs into a small bowl, making sure to remove any shell.

2 Mix well with a fork and then add the milk or cream and season. Mix again.

3 Take a small saucepan and add a knob of butter. Melt it over a low to medium heat. Make your toast!

4 Once the butter has melted, add the egg mixture. Leave for 30 seconds and then, using a wooden spoon, gently scrape the egg from the sides of the pan to the centre. Leave for 10 seconds and scrape again.

5 Repeat until the eggs are almost set, but are still runny. This will take 3–4 minutes. Then remove from the heat.

6 Give the eggs one last stir and serve immediately on buttered toast.

New Potato and Pea Frittata

Frittata is an Italian dish and can be eaten either hot or cold.

I definitely prefer to be cool!

Frittatas are a great way to add other ingredients to eggs. A frittata is cooked in the oven, or under the grill, and is very filling as it includes potatoes.

Ingredients

200g new potatoes
1 tablespoon olive oil
1 onion
100g frozen peas
6 eggs
50g cheddar cheese, grated
Salt and pepper

You will need a saucepan and an oven-safe frying pan.

ALLERGIES

Dairy, eggs

VEGETARIAN

NUMBER OF 4 SERVINGS

TIMINGS 30 MINUTES

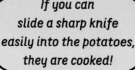
If you can slide a sharp knife easily into the potatoes, they are cooked!

Method

1 Cut the potatoes into quarters and put in a medium saucepan half full of cold water. Bring to the boil and cook the potatoes for 4–5 minutes.

2 While the potatoes cook, heat the oil in an oven-safe frying pan. Chop your onion into small pieces and add to the pan. Cook over a medium heat, stirring occasionally, for 5 minutes until softened.

3 Add the frozen peas to the potatoes and cook for 1 minute. Then strain the vegetables through a colander.

4 Turn the grill on high. Crack the eggs into a large jug and beat well, adding salt and pepper to season. Add half the cheese to the egg mixture.

5 Pour the egg and cheese mixture over the onions. Then spoon the potatoes and peas on top, spreading evenly across the pan. Cook for 5 minutes on a gentle heat.

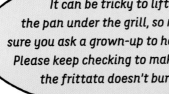

It can be tricky to lift the pan under the grill, so make sure you ask a grown-up to help you! Please keep checking to make sure the frittata doesn't burn!

6 Finally, top with the remaining cheese and place under the grill for 5 minutes. Serve hot or cold.

KEY INGREDIENT
#2 Cheese

I love cheese!

Cheese is made from milk and comes in many different varieties. Almost every country in the world has their own type of cheese and they are all delicious! Cheese can be hard, soft, blue, creamy, crumbly...

Baked Camembert

VEGETARIAN · VEGETARIAN

Ingredients
1 Camembert cheese, weighing approximately 250g
Ciabatta bread or French bread stick

You will need an ovenproof dish with a lid, that the cheese will just fit in.

ALLERGIES
Dairy, gluten, wheat

NUMBER OF **2** SERVINGS — LUNCH

NUMBER OF **4** SERVINGS — SNACK

TIMINGS 40 MINUTES

This is the easiest lunch in the world – but tastes wonderful. It's best to eat with good friends, as you'll be fighting each other to get to the melted cheese!

Fun Facts

Cheese can be made from the milk of cows, buffalo, goats, sheep, reindeer, camels and yaks.

There are over 1,800 different varieties of cheese.

Cheese was discovered in an Egyptian tomb built over 3,300 years ago.

Method

1 Heat your oven to 160°C / 350°F or gas mark 4. Place the cheese into the ovenproof dish. Take a sharp knife and score the rind of the cheese.

2 Place the lid on the ovenproof dish and put in the oven. Bake for 20 minutes. Add the bread to the oven for 10 minutes. Remove the cheese and bread from the oven. Cut the bread into slices and serve.

Baked Feta

Ingredients

1 garlic clove
1 lime
400g feta cheese

1 teaspoon dried marjoram or thyme
1 teaspoon dried chilli flakes
3 tablespoons olive oil
Tortilla chips

You will need an ovenproof dish approx. 23cm in diameter.

ALLERGIES
Dairy, gluten, wheat

Feta cheese comes from Greece and is made from sheep milk. It has a crumbly texture and a sharp, tangy flavour.

 NUMBER OF **4** SERVINGS

SNACK

 TIMINGS **40 MINUTES**

Method

1 Heat your oven to 160°C / 350°F or gas mark 4. Peel and finely chop the garlic clove. Zest and juice the lime.

Use a grater to remove the green skin of the lime to make the lime zest, then chop the lime in half to juice it.

I think my way will be faster!

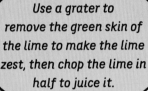

2 Crumble the feta cheese into the ovenproof dish. Sprinkle over the chopped garlic, dried herbs, lime zest and juice, chilli flakes and olive oil. Bake in the oven for 20 minutes.

Serve both cheeses with tortilla chips or bread.

Halloumi Burgers and Paneer Kebabs

Cheeses, such as Halloumi or paneer, hold their texture and shape when baked, so are perfect to use as the main ingredient in some of your favourite dishes.

Paneer cheese comes from India and is often used in curries. Halloumi cheese comes from Cyprus.

Hello you, too!

Halloumi Burgers

You can add whatever toppings you want to the Halloumi – onion rings, salad, salsa, hummus or avocado.

VEGETARIAN

Ingredients

1 large tomato
1 small lettuce
250g pack of Halloumi cheese
1 teaspoon olive oil
4 burger buns
Tomato salsa (see page 32)

You will need a baking tray and a frying pan.

ALLERGIES

Dairy, gluten, wheat

NUMBER OF 4 SERVINGS

TIMINGS 15 MINUTES

Method

1 Prepare your lettuce and tomato first by cutting the tomato into four slices horizontally, then by washing four crunchy lettuce leaves and drying with kitchen paper.

2 Divide the Halloumi into eight thick slices. Brush each slice with olive oil.

3 Heat a frying pan on high and add the cheese slices to the pan. Cook them for 3 minutes on each side until they have turned a golden colour.

4 Split open your burger buns and lightly toast under the grill on the cut side.

5 Assemble your burgers. Bun base, then lettuce, then tomato slice, then two slices of Halloumi cheese. Take the bun lid, spread a teaspoon of tomato salsa on the lid and place on top of the burger. Serve immediately.

Tandoori Paneer Kebabs

These are really simple to make and especially delicious!
Kebabs are normally made from small cubes of meat
or vegetables, and are cooked over a fire on a skewer.

En garde –
I have a sword!

Sheesh!

Ingredients

150g natural yoghurt, plus
50g for garnish

2 tablespoons tandoori
paste

1 tablespoon lemon juice

2 x 225g blocks of paneer

2 courgettes

1 red pepper
1 small red onion
Flatbreads or pitta breads

You will need four metal
or wooden skewers and
a baking tray.

ALLERGIES
Dairy, gluten, wheat

NUMBER OF **4** SERVINGS

TIMINGS **30 MINUTES**

If you are using wooden skewers, make sure they have been soaked in water for 10 minutes before using, otherwise they might burn.

Method

1 Heat the grill on high. Mix
the yoghurt, tandoori paste
and lemon juice in a bowl.

2 Chop each block of paneer into
eight cubes (3cm each) and add to
the spicy yoghurt mix, making sure
each piece of cheese is coated.

3 Slice the courgettes into eight pieces each, and
chop the pepper and onion into eight pieces.
Thread the cheese and vegetables onto the
skewers alternating between the ingredients.
There should be four pieces of cheese, four
pieces of courgette and two pieces each of
onion and pepper on every skewer.

Cut the outer layers of the onion into big squares!

Mind your fingers when you push the skewers through the cheese and vegetables!

4 Place the skewers on
a foil-lined baking tray
and cook under the grill
for 13–15 minutes.

5 Remove from the grill and serve
immediately with flatbreads and yoghurt.

Don't forget to turn the skewers over halfway through the cooking time!

Easy Cheese and Spinach Soufflé

Soufflés get their name from the French verb to blow or puff. They are light and airy (from the egg whites), and can be sweet or savoury. This savoury version is made with Gruyère cheese which comes from Switzerland, but you could use cheddar cheese instead. The recipe also uses Parmesan from Italy.

> We don't need one of those!

Ingredients

50g butter, plus some for greasing
30g Parmesan, grated
225g frozen chopped spinach
3 tablespoons plain flour
200ml milk

Salt and pepper
3 eggs, plus one extra egg white
115g Gruyère cheese

You will need a saucepan and a 1.3 litre soufflé dish.

ALLERGIES

Dairy, eggs, gluten, wheat

NUMBER OF **4** SERVINGS

TIMINGS **1 HOUR**

> To make this recipe vegetarian, replace the Parmesan with a vegetarian hard cheese.

Method

1 Heat the oven to 170°C / 375°F or gas mark 5. Grease the soufflé dish with butter and sprinkle with the grated Parmesan.

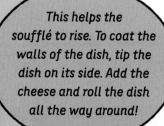

> This helps the soufflé to rise. To coat the walls of the dish, tip the dish on its side. Add the cheese and roll the dish all the way around!

2 Defrost the frozen spinach in a microwave and squeeze through a sieve to get rid of any excess moisture.

3 Melt the butter in a large saucepan on a medium heat, add the spinach and cook for a few minutes. Stir in the flour and cook gently for 1 minute until it has been absorbed.

4 Remove the pan from the heat, and gradually add the milk, stirring all the time. Season with salt and pepper. Return the pan to the heat and bring to the boil slowly, while stirring, until the mixture has thickened. Then remove from the heat to cool slightly.

5 Separate the eggs carefully into yolks and whites (see page 110 for tips on how to separate your eggs). Add the egg yolks to the pan, one at a time, while stirring. Add 90g of the Gruyère cheese to the pan and stir again.

6 In a mixing bowl, whisk the egg whites until they are stiff enough to stick to the bowl. Take a large spoonful of egg white and mix into the cheese and spinach mixture to loosen it. Then tip the remaining egg whites into the pan and fold in with a metal spoon.

'Folding in' means to gently scoop the mixture over the egg whites and cut through with a spoon, turn the bowl and repeat until all combined.

Don't think my egg whites were stiff enough!

7 Scrape the soufflé mixture into the greased soufflé dish, sprinkle with the remaining cheese and place in the oven on a baking tray.

8 Bake in the oven for 30 minutes until well risen.

CORE SKILL
#1 Soup

Soups can be chunky or smooth – it's really up to you! But to make a soup really smooth, you will need to use a handheld blender or a liquidiser!

I think I forgot to put the lid on!

Soup is an easy meal to make when you're in a hurry, or fancy something comforting! It's a great way to include lots of vegetables too.

Tomato Soup

Ingredients
1 onion

1 garlic clove

2 tablespoons olive oil

1 tablespoon tomato purée

400g tin of chopped tomatoes

600ml milk

Salt and pepper

You will need a large saucepan and a handheld blender or liquidiser.

ALLERGIES
Dairy

 NUMBER OF 4 SERVINGS

 TIMINGS 30 MINUTES

 VEGETARIAN VEGETARIAN

Method

1 Peel and chop the onion and garlic into small pieces.

2 Heat the olive oil in the pan on a medium heat and add the onion and garlic. Cook for 5 minutes until the onion has softened.

3 Add the tomato purée and tin of chopped tomatoes and bring to the boil, stirring. Turn the heat down and simmer for 15 minutes. Using your blender in the pan, blitz the tomato mixture until the soup is smooth.

4 Add the milk and bring up to the boil again.

Be careful with the blender as the soup will be very hot.

If you have a liquidiser, tip the tomato mixture into the jug and make sure you put the lid on!

24

Chilli Butternut Squash Soup

Ingredients

1 tablespoon olive oil

1 large onion

½ teaspoon mild chilli powder

700g butternut squash or pumpkin

750ml vegetable stock

Salt and pepper

You will need a large saucepan with a lid, a potato masher and handheld blender or liquidiser.

VEGETARIAN VEGETARIAN

NUMBER OF **4** SERVINGS

TIMINGS 40 MINUTES

Method

1 Peel and chop the onion into small pieces. Heat the oil in the pan on a medium heat and cook the onion for 5 minutes until softened. Add the chilli powder and cook for another 2 minutes.

2 Peel the squash with a vegetable peeler. Cut the squash in half lengthways and remove the seeds. Chop the squash into 2cm cubes. Add the squash to the pan and cook for 5 minutes before adding the vegetable stock.

Ask a grown-up to help you with this bit!

3 Bring to the boil and simmer for 15 minutes, covered. Using the potato masher to begin with, squish the squash into the soup to break down the cubes. Then use the blender in the pan to blitz the liquid until the soup is smooth.

I'll do the monster mash!

Season both soups and serve with crusty bread.

You can use basil as a garnish on the tomato soup, and a pinch of paprika for the squash!

Minestrone Soup

Minestrone soup comes from Italy. Traditionally it was made to use up lots of vegetables. It is a hearty soup packed with pasta or rice to make it as filling as possible. You can include whatever vegetables you like, but common ingredients include tomatoes, beans, onions, celery and carrots.

Ingredients

2 carrots
3 celery sticks
1 onion
1 garlic clove
2 tablespoons olive oil

2 large potatoes
2 tablespoons tomato purée
1 litre vegetable stock
400g chopped tomatoes
400g cannellini beans
100g spaghetti

Salt and pepper

You will need a large saucepan.

ALLERGIES

Gluten, wheat

VEGETARIAN VEGETARIAN

NUMBER OF 4 SERVINGS

TIMINGS 40 MINUTES

Method

1 First prepare the vegetables. Peel and chop the carrots and celery lengthways, and then into small pieces.

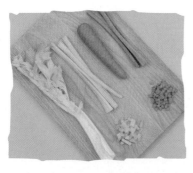

Peel the onion. Chop it in half and place flat side down onto the board. Then take your knife and finely chop the onion into small pieces.

Peel and finely chop the garlic.

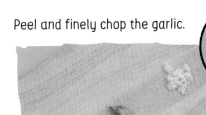

Take your time over this and mind your fingers!

This combination of vegetables is called a mirepoix in French or soffritto in Italian and is used in many recipes as the base flavour.

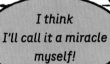

I think I'll call it a miracle myself!

2 Heat the olive oil in a large saucepan and add the chopped vegetables. Cook for 5 minutes until softened. Peel and chop the potatoes into 1cm pieces. Add to the pan and cook for another 5 minutes.

3 Add the tomato purée, tin of chopped tomatoes and stock, and stir. Bring to the boil, reduce the heat and simmer for 10 minutes.

4 Snap the spaghetti into pieces approximately 5cm in length and add to the pan along with the beans.

5 Cook for a further 10 minutes. Season and serve with warm crusty bread.

Did you know that it's almost impossible to snap a piece of spaghetti into only two pieces – there are nearly always three!

Crab and Sweetcorn Chowder and Cullen Skink

Seafood chowder is popular in the USA, particularly in New England. Cullen skink originated in Scotland and uses smoked haddock.

Cullen STINK – I don't want to taste that!

Both these fish soups start with the same basic recipe which makes a lovely creamy soup stuffed full of delicious fish!

Ingredients
Basic recipe:
15g butter
1 onion
400g potatoes (2 large ones)
500ml milk
2 spring onions

For the Cullen Skink:
500g smoked haddock (undyed frozen is fine if defrosted)

For the Chowder:
175g white crab meat (tinned is fine)
175g frozen sweetcorn

You will need a large saucepan and a large frying pan.

ALLERGIES
Dairy, shellfish

NUMBER OF **4** SERVINGS

TIMINGS **40 MINUTES**

Method
For the Cullen Skink only:

1 Place the smoked haddock in the frying pan with the milk and bring to the boil. Remove from the heat, cover and leave for about 5 minutes until the fish is cooked.

2 Using a slotted spoon, lift the fish out of the milk, flake it apart and keep separate.

Don't throw away the milk as you'll need it for the soup.

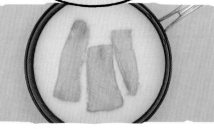

For both recipes:

3 Peel and chop the onion. Melt the butter in the saucepan over a medium heat. Add the onion and cook until softened for about 6–8 minutes.

4 Peel the potatoes and chop into 1cm cubes. Add to the pan and cook for 5 minutes, stirring to stop the potato sticking to the pan.

5 Add the milk (cooking milk for Cullen Skink) and bring to the boil. Reduce the heat and simmer for 15 minutes until the potato has cooked. Stir occasionally.

6 Now it's time to add the fish. For the chowder, add the crab and sweetcorn to the pan and cook for 2 minutes. For the Cullen Skink, add the flaked haddock and cook gently for 2 minutes. Finely slice the spring onions. Ladle the soup into bowls and sprinkle with the onions.

Serve immediately with crusty bread.

Doesn't it smell delicious?

I still think it smells fishy to me!

CORE SKILL
#2 Dips

Not that kind of dip, Llama!

Hummus

Hummus is made from chickpeas and comes from the Middle Eastern region of the Levant.

VEGETARIAN VEGETARIAN

Ingredients

400g tin of chickpeas
1 lemon
1 garlic clove
70ml olive oil
2 tablespoons tahini
Salt and pepper

You will need a food processor.

Tahini is a paste made from sesame seeds.

NUMBER OF **4** SERVINGS

TIMINGS **10 MINUTES**

Method

1 Drain the tin of chickpeas into a sieve and rinse with cold water.

2 Zest and juice the lemon. Peel and slice the garlic clove.

3 Put all the ingredients into the large bowl of the food processor and blitz until almost smooth. Add 30ml of water and blitz again for 2 minutes.

If the hummus looks too thick, add a little more water and blitz again!

4 Season and scrape into a bowl. Serve with carrot sticks and pitta bread.

Here are some really simple and tasty vegetarian dips to share with your friends when you fancy a snack. Eat them with fresh vegetables, breadsticks or tortilla chips! You can also use them in sandwiches, or as garnishes for main courses such as burgers (page 90) or chilli (page 93).

Guacamole

This avocado dip comes from Mexico and tastes delicious with tortilla chips!

VEGETARIAN
VEGETARIAN

Ingredients

2 ripe avocados
1 lime
¼ small red onion
1 bunch coriander
½ red chilli
Salt and pepper

NUMBER OF **4** SERVINGS

TIMINGS **10 MINUTES**

Method

Ask a grown-up to help you with this bit!

1 Cut the avocados in half and then in half again lengthways. Carefully ease the avocado away from the stone. Scoop out the flesh and place in a mixing bowl.

2 Squeeze the lime and tip the juice into the bowl. Finely chop the red onion and add to the bowl.

3 Finely chop the coriander and add to the bowl. Cut the chilli in half and scrape out the seeds. Chop the chilli into thin strips and then tiny pieces, and add to the mixture.

4 Season with salt and pepper, then take a potato masher and mash the ingredients together. Serve with tortilla chips.

Wash your hands once you've finished with the chilli and don't rub your eyes!

You could have told me sooner!

31

Tomato Salsa

Salsa also comes from Mexico and is eaten with tacos or tortilla chips. It's great on a burger too!

Ingredients

6 medium tomatoes
½ red onion
1 garlic clove
½ bunch coriander or parsley
½ tablespoon white wine vinegar

½ lime, juiced
Salt and pepper

NUMBER OF **4** SERVINGS

TIMINGS **25 MINUTES**

VEGETARIAN VEGETARIAN

Method

1 To remove the skin from the tomatoes, make a small slit in each tomato and put in a large bowl. Cover with boiling water, then leave for 15 minutes, or until the tomato skin starts to wrinkle.

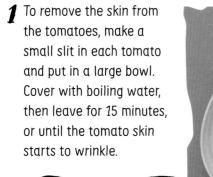

Be careful with the hot water!

2 Once cool, peel off the tomato skin with a sharp knife. Cut into halves, then deseed the tomatoes before chopping into small pieces. Place in a mixing bowl.

3 Chop the red onion, garlic and coriander or parsley into small pieces and add to the bowl.

4 Add the lime juice and white wine vinegar, then season with salt and pepper. Mix.

Tzatziki

This yoghurt dip is found in the Mediterranean and Middle East and is often eaten as a *meze* or appetiser.

Ingredients

½ cucumber

1 garlic clove

1 small bunch mint

200g natural or Greek-style yoghurt

Salt and pepper

NUMBER OF **4** SERVINGS

TIMINGS **10 MINUTES**

VEGETARIAN VEGETARIAN

Method

1 Cut the cucumber in half lengthways. Take a teaspoon and run it down the centre to remove the seeds. Then grate the remaining cucumber on the large side of the grater. Tip into a clean tea towel and squeeze out the juice.

2 Peel and crush the garlic clove. Finely chop the mint leaves. Put all the ingredients in a bowl and mix well. Season.

Don't use the mint stalk – it will be tough to eat.

Serve all the dips with pitta bread, vegetables, tortilla chips or breadsticks.

CORE SKILL
#3 Things on Toast

We've been eating toast since we worked out that if we held a slice of bread over the fire, it tasted better. Even better than toast, is toast with toppings! Perfect for a quick lunch or supper, generally most things taste nicer on top of toast!

I'm not sure about that. This tastes really prickly!

I have no words.

Cheese on Toast

Ingredients
2 thick slices of white bread

Butter, softened

100g cheddar cheese

1 teaspoon mustard (optional)

2 slices of ham (optional)

Small bunch chives (optional)

You will need a baking tray.

ALLERGIES
Dairy, gluten, wheat

TIMINGS 10 MINUTES

NUMBER OF **2** SERVINGS

Or one if you're very hungry!

Method

1 Preheat the grill on high. Take a baking tray and lay the bread slices on top. Put the tray under the grill to toast one side of the bread only. Grate the cheese.

2 Remove the toast from the grill. Butter the untoasted side. Spread the mustard on each slice of toast. Lay ham on top of the mustard. Then divide the cheese equally between the two slices.

3 Grill the cheese until it has melted and started to bubble. Remove and sprinkle with chives if using.

Be careful when using a grill, they get very hot!

Avocado on Toast With a Poached Egg

You could use the guacamole recipe on page 31 if you want a spicier flavour, or follow the simple recipe below!

Ingredients

2 thick slices of white bread

1 ripe large avocado

½ lemon, juiced

½ teaspoon smoked paprika (optional)

2 eggs

VEGETARIAN VEGETARIAN

You will need a saucepan.

ALLERGIES
Eggs, gluten, wheat

NUMBER OF **2** SERVINGS

TIMINGS 15 MINUTES

Fun Facts

An avocado is a fruit.

In Brazil, avocados are used to make ice cream.

Avocados are an Aztec symbol of love.

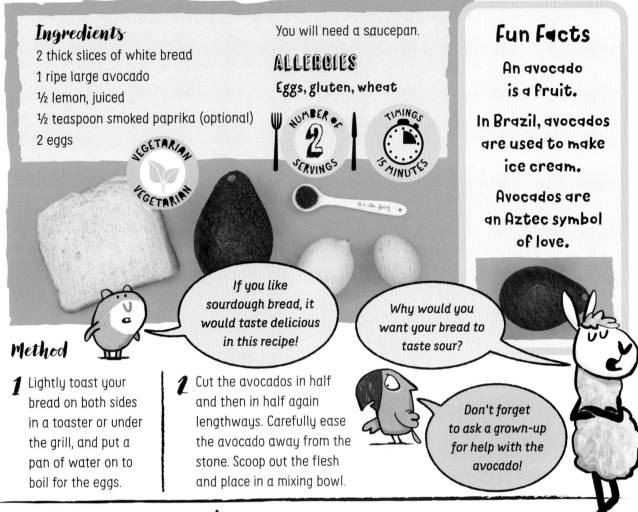

If you like sourdough bread, it would taste delicious in this recipe!

Why would you want your bread to taste sour?

Don't forget to ask a grown-up for help with the avocado!

Method

1 Lightly toast your bread on both sides in a toaster or under the grill, and put a pan of water on to boil for the eggs.

2 Cut the avocados in half and then in half again lengthways. Carefully ease the avocado away from the stone. Scoop out the flesh and place in a mixing bowl.

3 Squeeze the lemon juice over the avocado, add the paprika (if using) and using a fork, mash into a paste. Season with salt and pepper.

4 Poach the eggs, following the instructions on page 14. Drain them on kitchen paper.

5 Spread half the avocado mix onto each slice of toast, and top with an egg.

Garlic Mushrooms on Toast

Mushrooms on toast works well for brunch or a supper dish. It might look like a lot of mushrooms, but they cook down quickly as they contain a lot of water.

To make this recipe vegetarian, replace the Parmesan with a vegetarian hard cheese.

Ingredients

1 garlic clove
1 large shallot
40g butter
1 tablespoon olive oil
400g mushrooms
50ml double cream
Salt and pepper
50g Parmesan, grated
2 thick slices of white bread

You will need a frying pan.

ALLERGIES

Dairy, gluten, wheat

NUMBER OF **2** SERVINGS

TIMINGS **20** MINUTES

A shallot is a member of the onion family, but has a slightly sweeter flavour. If you don't have one, use half a small onion instead.

Method

1 Crush the garlic clove and finely chop the shallot. Melt the butter with the oil in the frying pan on a medium heat, and add the garlic and onion. Cook for 2–3 minutes.

2 Remove the stalks and skin of the mushrooms, or wipe with a cloth, before slicing. Add to the pan, increase the heat and cook for 4–5 minutes.

3 Add the cream to the pan, season and let the sauce bubble for 2 minutes.

4 Lightly toast the bread, spoon half the mushrooms over each slice and sprinkle with Parmesan.

French Toast With Bacon

French toast, or eggy bread, or *pain perdu* in French, can be sweet or savoury. Here, it's served with bacon for a delicious breakfast.

If you add maple syrup, it can be sweet AND savoury!

Pain perdu means forgotten bread!

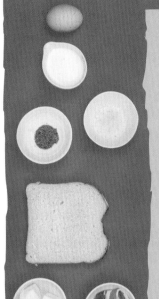

Ingredients

2 eggs
150ml milk
Salt and pepper
4 thick slices white bread
30g butter
4 smoked streaky bacon rashers
50ml maple syrup (optional)

You will need a frying pan, a baking tray and a wide flat-bottomed dish.

ALLERGIES

Dairy, eggs, gluten, wheat

NUMBER OF **2** SERVINGS

TIMINGS **20 MINUTES**

Method

1 Break the eggs into a wide dish, add the milk and seasoning, and whisk together.

2 Put two slices of bread into the egg mixture and turn them over. Leave to absorb for 1 minute. Heat the grill on high.

3 Melt half the butter in a frying pan, over a medium heat. Take the slices from the egg mixture and add them to the pan. Cook for 3–4 minutes on each side.

4 While cooking, soak the remaining bread slices in the egg mixture. Put the bacon on a baking tray and cook under the grill, remembering to turn the rashers over halfway through.

Keep the cooked toast warm in the oven covered in foil!

5 Cook the remaining bread slices. Serve with two rashers of bacon.

Don't forget the maple syrup!

KEY INGREDIENT
#3 Pasta

Pasta comes from Italy. There are over 1,000 different varieties of pasta in many different shapes, textures and flavours. It is made from flour and water, sometimes with egg, and can be dried or fresh. In 1957, a BBC news programme called *Panorama* showed a family harvesting spaghetti from a tree as an April Fool's joke.

I told you I was a spaghetti tree!

If you learn how to make spaghetti Bolognese and macaroni cheese, you get a bonus recipe because you can then make lasagne too!

Spaghetti Bolognese

Ingredients

1 tablespoon olive oil
500g beef mince
1 onion
2 sticks of celery
1 carrot
1 garlic clove
2 tablespoons tomato purée
300ml chicken stock
Salt and pepper
300g dried spaghetti
50g Parmesan, grated

Bolognese sauce, or ragu, comes from the Italian city of Bologna. Italians don't serve spaghetti with Bolognese ragu, but the rest of the world certainly does!

You will need two large saucepans or casseroles.

ALLERGIES

Dairy, gluten, wheat

NUMBER OF 4 SERVINGS

TIMINGS 45 MINUTES

Method

1 Heat the saucepan on a medium heat, and add the olive oil. Add the mince to the pan and break it up with a wooden spoon. Brown the mince in the pan, until it is all caramelised.

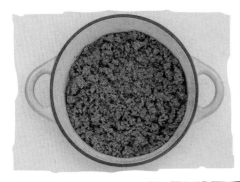

2 Finely chop the onion, celery, carrot and garlic clove.

Be careful using the knife!

3 Add the vegetables to the mince and stir. Cook for 5 minutes until the vegetables have softened. Add the tomato purée and stir again.

4 Add the chicken stock and season. Stir. Cook over a medium heat for 20 minutes until the stock has reduced to a thick sauce. Season with salt and pepper.

You can take the sauce off the heat now and leave until you need it. You could also freeze it once cool to eat another day.

5 When you are ready to eat, fill a large pan with boiling water, a pinch of salt and a dribble of olive oil. Add 300g spaghetti to the pan. Bring the water to the boil and cook for 8–10 minutes until the spaghetti is cooked al dente.

Al dente means 'still firm when bitten'. Overcooked spaghetti is not very nice!

6 Reheat the Bolognese sauce if necessary, strain the pasta and divide it into four bowls. Spoon the sauce over the pasta and sprinkle with Parmesan.

Macaroni Cheese

Macaroni cheese is very versatile. Once you have learnt the basic sauce recipe, you can add anything you like to the mix – vegetables, bacon, or even lobster!

VEGETARIAN VEGETARIAN

Substitute the Parmesan cheese with a vegetarian hard cheese to make this vegetarian.

Ingredients

200g cheddar cheese

50g Parmesan

50g butter

50g plain flour

1 teaspoon mustard powder

600ml milk

350g macaroni or any other dried pasta shapes

50g breadcrumbs

Salt and pepper

You will need two large saucepans and an ovenproof dish approximately 25cm x 18cm.

ALLERGIES

Dairy, gluten, wheat

NUMBER OF **4** SERVINGS

TIMINGS **45 MINUTES**

Method

1 Heat the oven to 170°C / 375°F or gas mark 5. Grate both cheeses.

2 To make the cheese sauce, put the butter, flour, mustard powder and milk in a large pan and heat on the hob. Use a whisk to mix the ingredients together as the butter melts. Keep stirring as the sauce thickens and comes to the boil, then simmer for 10 minutes.

3 Once the sauce has cooked, add 175g of cheddar cheese to the pan so it melts, and take off the heat.

4 While the sauce is cooking, cook the macaroni until *al dente* (about 10 minutes). Strain the pasta, and put back in the pan. Tip the cheese sauce into the pasta pan and mix.

5 Tip the mixture into the ovenproof dish and sprinkle over the remaining cheeses and breadcrumbs. Bake in the oven for 20 minutes.

Delicious!

Lasagne

Lasagne is a layered baked pasta dish made using the Bolognese and cheese sauces from the previous two recipes.

Easy peasy! Erm... which comes first again?

Ingredients

1 portion cheese sauce
200g dried lasagne sheets
1 portion Bolognese sauce
50g cheddar cheese
50g Parmesan

You will need an ovenproof dish and a large baking tray.

ALLERGIES

Dairy, gluten, wheat

 NUMBER OF **6** SERVINGS

 TIMINGS 1 HOUR 40 MINUTES

Method

You might need to snap the sheets into different shapes.

1 Heat the oven to 170°C / 375°F or gas mark 5.

2 Using a ladle, take a ladleful of cheese sauce and spread it on the bottom of the lasagne dish.

3 Cover the sauce with a layer of lasagne sheets.

Like this, you mean?

4 Cover the sheets with half the Bolognese sauce, making sure you have an even layer. Then ladle over a third of the cheese sauce. Add another layer of lasagne sheets. Repeat with the rest of the Bolognese and half the remaining cheese sauce.

5 Add a final layer of lasagne, the last of the cheese sauce and sprinkle both cheeses on top.

6 Place on the baking tray and cook in the oven for 45 minutes.

Keep an eye on the lasagne. If it starts to look too brown, cover with foil until the time is up.

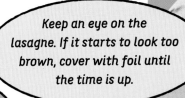

Garlic Prawn Linguine

Really quick and easy to make, this is a light and summery dish. You can use whatever green vegetables you have in your fridge. This recipe uses peas and asparagus.

You can also use whatever pasta you have – this is a really flexible dish!

I'm really flexible too!

Ingredients

100g asparagus
2 garlic cloves
300g linguine
100g frozen peas
75g butter

175g frozen raw king prawns, defrosted
½ lemon
Salt and pepper

You will need a frying pan and a large saucepan.

ALLERGIES
Dairy, gluten, shellfish, wheat

 NUMBER OF **4** SERVINGS

 TIMINGS **20 MINUTES**

Fun Facts

Garlic is a member of the onion family.

It is actually very good for you, even if it can give you smelly breath.

Garlic keeps mosquitoes away.

I thought it was vampires!

Method

1 Snap off the tough end of each asparagus stem. Cut each of the remaining stems into three pieces. Peel and finely chop the garlic.

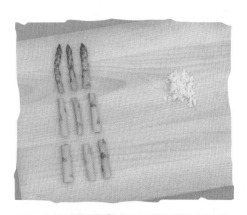

2 Put a large pan of water on to boil and add the pasta. Cook for 7 minutes and then add the vegetables.

3 Cook for a further 3 minutes and then remove from the heat and strain through a colander. Keep covered so the pasta and vegetables stay warm.

4 Melt the butter in a frying pan and, once foaming, add the chopped garlic. Cook on a medium heat for 2 minutes, then add the prawns, stirring until the prawns turn pink and are cooked through. Remove from the heat.

This won't take very long!

5 Squeeze the lemon juice over the prawns and season with salt and pepper. Tip the pasta and vegetables into the frying pan and stir to coat in the buttery garlic sauce.

6 Serve immediately with a salad or crusty bread.

I love garlic!

We know!

KEY INGREDIENT
#4 Noodles

Noodles can be made from different things... Udon from wheat, soba from buckwheat – you can even have noodles made from rice!

I look like a noodle!

Noodles are used in most Asian cooking and are made from flour and water. The dough is rolled flat and cut, or stretched into long strips. Like pasta, noodles can be cooked in boiling water, but they can also be fried...

Pork Chow Mein

Chow mein means 'stir-fried noodles' and is quick and easy to make. You can add any meat or fish to the dish; we're using pork in this recipe!

Traditionally, a stir-fry is cooked in a wok, but a frying pan over a high heat will work too.

Ingredients
225g dried egg noodles
1 tablespoon sesame oil
1 garlic clove
1 thumb-sized piece of ginger
1 small head broccoli

3 spring onions
2 tablespoons dark soy sauce
200g pork fillet
2 tablespoons vegetable oil

You will need a wok or a frying pan.

ALLERGIES
Eggs, gluten, wheat

NUMBER OF **4** SERVINGS

TIMINGS **15 MINUTES**

Method

1 Cook the noodles in a pan of boiling water according to the packet instructions (normally 5-10 minutes). Once cooked, strain and return to the pan with the sesame oil. Stir and keep covered.

1 Peel and finely chop the garlic and ginger. Slice the spring onions into small pieces. Cut up the broccoli into small pieces, removing the thick stalks.

3 Cut the pork fillet into thin strips. Heat the wok on a high heat and add 1 tablespoon of vegetable oil. Add the pork to the pan and stir. Once the meat has browned, remove from the heat and put in a bowl. Wipe out the pan.

Be careful as the pan will be very hot!

4 Put the pan back on a medium heat. Add the remaining vegetable oil, garlic, ginger and spring onions to the pan. Cook for 2 minutes, then add the broccoli. Increase the heat to high. Cook for 2 more minutes, then add the pork back to the pan, and add the soy sauce. Cook for 1 more minute.

5 Finally add the noodles to the pan, stir until coated in the sauce and serve.

Now that's what I call fast food!

Sesame Beef Noodles

This quick and easy beef dish has lots of flavour, but is also really healthy.

A good way to work on your stir-fry technique!

Ingredients

225g dried egg noodles
1 tablespoon sesame oil
350g lean rump steak
100g green beans
1 courgette

4 spring onions
1 tablespoon vegetable oil
2 tablespoons runny honey
2 teaspoons sesame seeds
2 tablespoons dark soy sauce

You will need a wok or deep-sided frying pan with a lid, and a saucepan.

ALLERGIES

Eggs, gluten, wheat

NUMBER OF **4** SERVINGS

TIMINGS **15 MINUTES**

This recipe will work with chicken too.

Method

1 Cook the noodles in a pan of boiling water according to the packet instructions (usually 5–10 minutes). Once cooked, strain and return to the pan with the sesame oil. Stir and keep covered.

2 Finely slice the steak into thin strips, and season.

3 Prepare your vegetables. Chop the beans in half. Chop the courgette in half lengthways, then into 1cm pieces. Slice the spring onions.

4 Heat the wok on a high heat and add half of the vegetable oil. Add the beef strips and stir-fry for 2 minutes.

Don't stir the beef immediately – let it start to brown before moving it around in the pan!

5 Add the sesame seeds and cook for 1 minute, then add the honey. Make sure the beef is coated and then add half the soy sauce to make a sticky sauce. Remove from the pan and keep warm.

I can do this bit, honest!

6 Wipe out the wok and heat the remaining vegetable oil over a high heat. Add the courgette, beans and 2 tablespoons of water and replace the lid. Steam fry the vegetables for 2 minutes. Remove the lid and add the spring onions. Stir-fry for 2 minutes.

Be careful of the steam when you take off the lid.

7 Add the noodles and 1 tablespoon of the soy sauce to the wok and toss with the vegetables.

8 Divide the noodles and vegetables into four, add the beef and serve immediately.

Try eating your noodles with chopsticks!

Vegetarian Singapore Noodles

VEGETARIAN VEGETARIAN

Turmeric is a yellow spice, which is also used as a dye. It can stain if it gets wet.

This dish is made using rice noodles, or *vermicelli*, and curry powder, which gives the noodles their signature 'takeaway' flavour. The recipe below is for a vegetarian version, but you can easily add cooked pork and prawns if you like.

Like this, you mean?

Ingredients

200g rice noodles
1 tablespoon sesame oil
1 tablespoon mild curry powder
½ teaspoon ground turmeric
1 teaspoon caster sugar
3 tablespoons dark soy sauce

1 tablespoon vegetable oil
1 green pepper
1 red pepper
2 carrots
100g baby sweetcorn
4 spring onions
100g bean sprouts

You will need a wok or large frying pan.

NUMBER OF **4** SERVINGS

TIMINGS 20 MINUTES

Method

1 Put the rice noodles in a large bowl and pour over boiling water. Make sure they are covered, and leave to soften for 5–10 minutes. Once ready, drain and return to the bowl with a teaspoon of the sesame oil.

The oil is to stop the noodles sticking together.

1 Mix the curry powder, turmeric, sugar, remaining sesame oil, soy sauce and 2 tablespoons of water in a bowl.

3 Prepare the vegetables by slicing the pepper and carrots into thin strips. Cut the sweetcorn in quarters lengthways and chop the spring onions into small pieces.

Ask a grown-up to help!

4 Heat the wok on a high heat. Add the vegetable oil, pepper, carrots and sweetcorn to the pan and stir-fry for 3–4 minutes until they have softened and started to caramelise.

If you want to add cooked pork or prawns, add them at this stage!

5 Add the noodles to the pan with the sauce, spring onions and bean sprouts. Stir-fry for 2–3 minutes.

6 Spoon into bowls and serve.

Ramen

I don't know about umami, but this is certainly yummy!

Ramen is a Japanese noodle soup, flavoured with savoury soy sauce or miso, which is a fermented soya bean paste. This savoury taste is called 'umami' and is the fifth taste that can be detected by our taste buds. The others are sweet, salty, sour and bitter.

Ingredients

4 eggs
3 garlic cloves
1 thumb-sized piece of ginger
700ml chicken stock
4 tablespoons dark soy sauce
375g ramen noodles

1 tablespoon sesame oil
2 cooked chicken breasts
100g baby spinach
50g baby sweetcorn
2 spring onions
2 tablespoons of sesame seeds

You will need a large stockpot and a large saucepan, or two large saucepans.

ALLERGIES

Eggs, gluten, wheat

NUMBER OF **4** SERVINGS

TIMINGS **30 MINUTES**

You can use different types of noodles if you don't have ramen noodles, but make sure they are medium or thick, not vermicelli.

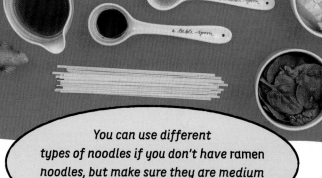

Method

1 Soft boil the eggs and set aside. (See page 12 for instructions.)

1 Peel the garlic and ginger and cut into large slices.

3 Put the chicken stock into a stockpot and add the chopped garlic, ginger and soy sauce to the pan. Bring to the boil and simmer for 10 minutes.

4 Cook the noodles in boiling water according to the packet instructions (usually 5–10 minutes). Once cooked, strain and put in a bowl with the sesame oil. Stir and keep covered.

5 Chop the chicken breast into slices. Peel the eggs and cut them in half. Chop the baby sweetcorn in half lengthways.

6 Take four bowls and divide the noodles between them. Top each with a quarter of the chicken, baby spinach, eggs and sweetcorn.

Arrange the toppings nicely so the food looks appealing!

7 Ladle the broth over the bowls and then sprinkle with chopped spring onions and sesame seeds.

To remove the garlic and ginger, you could strain the broth first through a sieve, but I just use a slotted spoon to fish out the bits.

Fishing? That sounds like a great idea!

Pad Thai

Tofu is made from bean curd and soaks up the pad Thai flavours beautifully.

I soak up things beautifully too!

Pad Thai is a national dish of Thailand which uses flat rice noodles and bean sprouts, as well as a tangy sauce made with fish sauce (*nam pla*) and lime juice. There are two versions here – one including chicken and prawn, and a vegetarian version using tofu.

Chicken and Prawn Pad Thai

Ingredients

200g flat rice noodles (5mm wide)

1 teaspoon sesame oil

2 teaspoons tamarind paste

3 tablespoons fish sauce

1 tablespoon soft brown sugar

1 lime, juiced, plus wedges to serve

¼ teaspoon chilli powder

4 spring onions

2 eggs

100g cooked chicken

2 tablespoons vegetable oil

100g cooked prawns

100g bean sprouts

2 tablespoons roasted salted peanuts

You will need a wok.

ALLERGIES

Eggs, nuts, shellfish

NUMBER OF **4** SERVINGS

TIMINGS **30** MINUTES

Method

1 Put the noodles in a large bowl and pour boiling water over them. Cover and allow to soak for 20 minutes, then drain. Put back in the bowl with a teaspoon of sesame oil and mix until coated.

2 Put the tamarind paste, fish sauce, sugar, lime juice and chilli powder in a bowl and mix together.

52

3 Chop the spring onions into small pieces. Crack the two eggs into a bowl and beat with a fork. Shred the chicken with two forks so it pulls apart.

4 Heat the wok on a high heat and add the vegetable oil. Add the spring onions and stir-fry for 1 minute. Move the onions to one side of the pan and then add the egg.

Be careful! The wok is very hot.

5 Stir-fry the egg so it starts to cook like an omelette. Add the prawns, shredded chicken, bean sprouts and noodles. Finally add the sauce and stir until everything is coated and heated through.

6 Divide into bowls and sprinkle with peanuts and wedges of lime.

Don't forget to check for nut allergies!

Vegetarian Pad Thai

Ingredients

300g firm tofu

3 tablespoons cornflour

4 tablespoons vegetable oil

200g flat rice noodles
  (5mm wide)

1 teaspoon sesame oil

2 teaspoons tamarind paste

3 tablespoons light soy sauce

1 tablespoon soft brown sugar

1 lime, juiced, plus wedges
  to serve

¼ teaspoon mild chilli powder

1 garlic clove

4 spring onions

2 eggs

100g bean sprouts

2 tablespoons roasted
  salted peanuts

You will need a wok and
a non-stick frying pan.

ALLERGIES

Eggs, nuts

NUMBER OF
4
SERVINGS

TIMINGS
40 MINUTES

*We are going to
cook the tofu by pan-frying
it in vegetable oil.*

*Make sure
a grown-up is available
to help you!*

Method

1 To prepare the tofu, dry it with kitchen paper, squeezing as much liquid out as you can. Cut into 2cm cubes. Coat each cube in cornflour, making sure each side is covered.

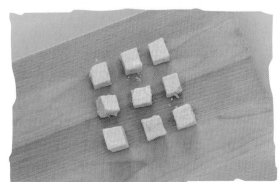

2 Heat 2 tablespoons of vegetable oil in a frying pan over a medium heat. Once the oil is hot, add the tofu to the pan, and cook for 3 minutes before turning onto another side. Repeat until all the sides of the tofu are golden-brown.

3 Remove from the pan and drain on kitchen paper.

4 Put the noodles in a large bowl and pour boiling water over them. Cover and allow to soak for 20 minutes, then drain. Put back in the bowl with the sesame oil and mix until coated. Put the tamarind paste, soy sauce, sugar, lime juice and chilli powder in a bowl and mix together.

This is easy peasy!

5 Chop the spring onions and garlic into small pieces. Crack the two eggs into a bowl and beat with a fork.

6 Heat the wok on a high heat and add the remaining vegetable oil. Stir-fry the spring onions for 1 minute. Move them to the side of the pan and then add the egg.

7 Stir-fry the egg so it starts to cook like an omelette. Add the fried tofu, bean sprouts and noodles. Finally add the sauce and stir until everything is coated and heated through.

8 Divide into bowls and sprinkle with peanuts and wedges of lime.

This is one of my favourites!

I thought I was your favourite!

CORE SKILL
#4 Salads

I like dressing up!

Not that kind of dressing, silly!

Salads are a great way to make sure that you're eating lots of fresh vegetables. You can put anything in a salad, but it's best to make them interesting with lots of different textures. A delicious dressing helps too!

Greek Salad

Ingredients
6 tomatoes

1 red onion

1 cucumber

100g feta cheese

16 black olives

2 tablespoons extra-virgin olive oil

½ tablespoon red wine vinegar or lemon juice

½ teaspoon dried oregano

Salt and pepper

You will need a salad bowl.

ALLERGIES
Dairy

VEGETARIAN
VEGETARIAN

NUMBER OF
4
SERVINGS

TIMINGS
15 MINUTES

Method

1 Chop the tomatoes into quarters. Chop the red onion in half and thinly slice. Cut the cucumber in half lengthways, scoop out the seeds with a spoon and then chop into bite-size pieces.

2 Place in a salad bowl with the feta cheese, crumbled, and the olives.

3 To make the dressing, mix the olive oil, red wine vinegar or lemon juice, oregano and salt and pepper together in a jug.

4 Pour over the salad and gently stir in!

> If you've got a clean jam jar, put the ingredients in the jar, tighten the lid and shake!

Chicken Caesar Salad

Ingredients

1 ciabatta loaf
3 tablespoons olive oil
2 teaspoons sea salt
2 cooked chicken breasts, or any leftover chicken (see page 76 for Roast Chicken)
1 large cos lettuce
50g Parmesan
1 garlic clove
2 anchovy fillets

5 tablespoons mayonnaise
1 tablespoon white wine vinegar

You will need a baking tray and a mortar and pestle.

ALLERGIES

Dairy, eggs, gluten, wheat

> Versions of mortars and pestles have been used to prepare food for centuries!

NUMBER OF **4** SERVINGS

TIMINGS 25 MINUTES

Method

1 Heat the oven to 180°C / 400°F or gas mark 6. Tear the ciabatta into 2cm pieces. Spread out on the baking tray and sprinkle with the olive oil.

2 Rub the bread into the oil to make sure it is all soaked up and then sprinkle with a little salt. Bake in the oven for 8–10 minutes, turning occasionally. Remove from the oven to cool.

3 Chop the cooked chicken breast into bite-size pieces. Prepare the lettuce by separating and washing the leaves, then chopping into pieces. Use a vegetable peeler to shave curls of Parmesan.

4 Make the dressing by crushing the garlic clove with the anchovies in the mortar and pestle.

I think I could be quite good at this!

5 Add the garlic mix to a bowl and mix in the mayonnaise and white wine vinegar.

Caesar dressing should be like yoghurt, so if your dressing is a bit thick, add a little water.

6 Arrange the ingredients in a salad bowl, or four individual bowls if you prefer, and drizzle with the dressing.

Potato salad and coleslaw are delicious side dishes to have with barbecue beef or chicken! They keep for a few days in the fridge too, so make double the recipe and enjoy some later!

Potato Salad

Ingredients

1kg medium potatoes
2 spring onions
4 tablespoons mayonnaise
2 teaspoons white wine vinegar
1 teaspoon salt
1 small bunch chives

You will need a saucepan and salad bowl.

ALLERGIES

Eggs

NUMBER OF **6** SERVINGS

TIMINGS 30 MINUTES

Waxy potatoes are best – Charlotte, Jersey Royals or Desiree are good varieties to use.

Method

1 Peel the potatoes and cut into 2–3cm chunks. Put the potatoes into a pan and cover with boiling water. Bring to the boil and then simmer for 10 minutes – or until a knife slips easily into the potato.

2 Drain the potatoes through a colander, and let cool. Chop the spring onions into small pieces.

3 In a large bowl, mix the mayonnaise and vinegar together, and season with the salt. Add the potatoes and spring onions, and mix again.

4 Chop the chives into small pieces and sprinkle over the salad.

Coleslaw

Ingredients

½ small white or red cabbage
3 carrots
1 small onion

2 tablespoons white wine vinegar
1 tablespoon mustard
6 tablespoons mayonnaise
Salt and pepper

ALLERGIES

Eggs

VEGETARIAN
VEGETARIAN

NUMBER OF 6 SERVINGS

TIMINGS 20 MINUTES

Method

1 Cut the core out of the cabbage half, and finely shred with either a sharp knife or using a food processor.

There's a lot of shredding in this recipe, but it's worth it!

Make sure you don't shred your fingers!

1 Grate the carrots on the large side of the grater, and finely slice the onion. Place all the vegetables into a large bowl.

I'm not very good at shredding!

3 Add the remaining ingredients and mix together so they are all coated in the dressing.

The next two salads work really well for parties or family gatherings and are healthy too! You can vary the amount of chilli in them depending on your taste.

Salads are tastier than exercise!

Black Bean and Sweetcorn Salsa

Ingredients

For the salsa:
3 tomatoes
160g tin of sweetcorn
230g tin of black beans
4 spring onions
1 small bunch coriander
1 green chilli

For the dressing:
1 garlic clove
½ green chilli
1 teaspoon sea salt
½ teaspoon ground cumin
½ lime, juiced
2 tablespoons olive oil
Black pepper to season

You will need a mortar and pestle and a salad bowl.

NUMBER OF **6** SERVINGS

TIMINGS **25** MINUTES

VEGETARIAN

Ask a grown-up to help with the chilli chopping!

Method

1 Pierce the skin of the tomatoes with a sharp knife and place in a bowl. Cover with boiling water and leave for 15 minutes until the skin starts to peel.

2 To make the dressing, finely chop the garlic clove and chilli, removing the chilli seeds.

To chop the chilli, take a sharp knife and cut lengthways from stalk to tip. Open the chilli out and scrape out the seeds. Finally, cut off the stalk, before chopping into strips, and then small pieces.

Make sure you wash your hands immediately and don't touch your eyes!

3 Put the garlic, chilli, salt and cumin into a mortar and pestle and crush. Then add the lime juice, oil and pepper and mix.

4 Slice the spring onions, and peel, chop and deseed the tomatoes. Roughly chop the coriander and slice the chilli.

5 Place all the salsa ingredients in a bowl, and pour over the dressing.

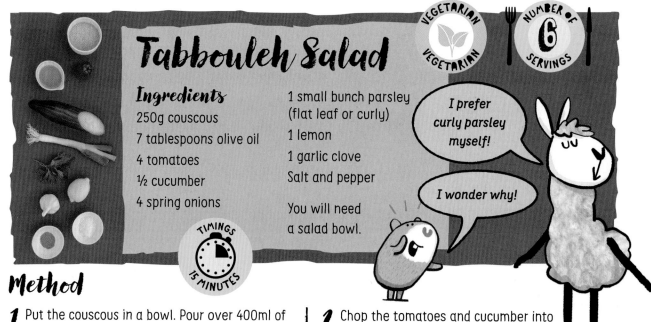

Tabbouleh Salad

Ingredients

250g couscous
7 tablespoons olive oil
4 tomatoes
½ cucumber
4 spring onions

1 small bunch parsley (flat leaf or curly)
1 lemon
1 garlic clove
Salt and pepper

You will need a salad bowl.

I prefer curly parsley myself!

I wonder why!

TIMINGS 15 MINUTES

Method

1 Put the couscous in a bowl. Pour over 400ml of boiling water and stir in 1 tablespoon of olive oil. Leave for 5 minutes until all the liquid has been absorbed. See page 73 for method.

2 Chop the tomatoes and cucumber into small pieces. Finely slice the spring onions, and chop the parsley.

Mind your fingers or ask a grown-up to help!

3 Zest the lemon. Using a fork, fluff up the couscous to separate the grains. Add the vegetables and lemon zest.

4 Crush the garlic clove and place in a jar or jug. Add the remaining 6 tablespoons of olive oil, 2 tablespoons of lemon juice and season well. Shake or stir well and drizzle over the couscous.

Serve in large sharing bowls so that people can help themselves.

KEY INGREDIENT
#5 Rice

Different rice types do different things. This risotto uses arborio rice as it contains a lot of starch, which makes the risotto creamy. Basmati rice has less starch and is fluffy once cooked.

Rice is probably the most widely-eaten food in the world. Easy to cook and add flavour to, nearly every nationality in the world has their own rice dish. There are hundreds of different varieties of rice including arborio, paella, basmati, sticky, brown, short grain, long grain, wild, black and jasmine...

Butternut Squash or Pumpkin Risotto

Risotto comes from Italy and is made by cooking rice slowly in stock, while stirring gently to release the starch. Once you know how to make a basic risotto, you can add any flavours you like.

Ingredients

1 butternut squash or medium pumpkin

1 teaspoon chilli powder

1 tablespoon sea salt

2 tablespoons olive oil

1.2 litres chicken stock (use vegetable if vegetarian)

100g chestnuts (optional)

1 large onion

2 garlic cloves

3 celery stalks

12 bacon rashers (optional)

45g butter

300g risotto rice

Salt and pepper

100g Parmesan

You will need a heavy-bottomed pan or casserole, a saucepan, a ladle, a plastic bag and a roasting tin.

ALLERGIES
Dairy

NUMBER OF **6** SERVINGS

TIMINGS 1 HOUR

Method

1 Heat your oven to 170°C / 375°F or gas mark 5.

2 Cut the butternut squash or pumpkin in half and scoop out the seeds. Separate the seeds from the flesh of the squash and rinse them.

We'll roast the seeds and use them to add texture to the final dish.

3 Cut the squash or pumpkin into large chunks. Place in a plastic bag with a tablespoon of olive oil, the sea salt and chilli powder. Shake together until the squash is coated evenly. Spread in a single layer on the baking tray and roast in the oven for 30 minutes.

4 Heat the stock in a large saucepan. Finely chop the onion and celery, and peel and chop the garlic.

5 In a heavy-bottomed pan, put the remaining tablespoon of olive oil and 15g of butter. Add the onions, celery and garlic to the pan and cook very slowly for 10 minutes until softened.

This is called 'sweating' the vegetables.

No, this is called 'sweating'.

6 Turn up the pan to high and add the rice. Keep stirring for 2 minutes as the rice starts to fry. Add a ladle of stock to the pan and stir. Once the first ladle of stock has evaporated, turn the heat down very low, and add another ladle of stock, plus a pinch of salt. Stir gently.

7 Keep adding stock, ladle by ladle, as it cooks into the rice, and keep stirring. After 20 minutes, test the rice. It should be soft, with a little bite. Check the seasoning too.

You need to be patient as this can take a little time!

8 When the squash has reached 30 minutes cooking time, take it out of the oven. Add the squash seeds, and chestnuts and bacon, if using, over the top of the squash.

Be careful as the roasting tin will be hot!

9 Put back in the oven for 10 minutes until the bacon is crisp. Once cooked, take out of the oven. Keep the bacon, chestnuts and seeds warm while you chop the squash up. Add the squash to the risotto and stir.

10 Remove the risotto from the heat. Add the remaining 30g of butter and the Parmesan and stir. Cover the pan with a lid and let the risotto rest for 3 minutes.

11 Finally, serve and scatter over the chestnuts, seeds and bacon rashers, with some extra grated Parmesan.

For a vegetarian dish, don't use bacon or chicken stock, and substitute the Parmesan cheese. To make this vegan, leave out the butter...

Can I have it all please?

Seafood Paella

Paella comes from Spain and contains lots of lovely ingredients including seafood, chorizo and peppers. The name paella comes from the wide shallow pan used to cook the dish. The Spanish have special paella pans, but a large frying pan will do the job nicely.

Chorizo is a spicy Spanish sausage flavoured with paprika.

Paprika is... What's paprika?

Paprika is a spice made from peppers. In Spain it's called pimenton.

Ingredients

- 2 tablespoons olive oil
- 200g cooking chorizo
- 4 skinless and boneless chicken thighs
- 1 red pepper
- 1 green pepper
- 3 garlic cloves
- 1 onion
- 1 small bunch flat leaf parsley
- Salt and pepper
- 1 small pinch saffron (optional)
- 300g paella rice
- 400g tin of chopped tomatoes
- 1 litre chicken or vegetable stock
- 100g frozen peas
- 175g frozen raw king prawns, defrosted
- 150g frozen raw squid, defrosted (optional)
- 1 lemon

You will need a large heavy-bottomed frying pan or shallow casserole at least 28cm in diameter.

ALLERGIES
Shellfish

NUMBER OF **6** SERVINGS

TIMINGS **45 MINUTES**

Saffron is a very expensive spice and comes from the crocus flower. It gives food a lovely yellow colour!

But be careful, it can stain!

Not again!

Method

1 Heat the olive oil on a medium heat in the frying pan. Chop the chorizo into slices about 1cm in size. Add to the pan and cook for 5 minutes, stirring occasionally. Chop the chicken thighs into 1cm strips, add to the pan and cook.

2 Cut the peppers in half and deseed. Roughly chop into bite-size pieces. Peel and chop the onion and garlic. Add to the pan and stir. Prepare the parsley by finely chopping the stalks and roughly chopping the leaves. Add the stalks to the pan and set the leaves aside until later.

3 Season with salt and pepper, and add the saffron, if using, to the pan. Cook the vegetables for 10 minutes until they have softened.

4 Add the rice and stir through the vegetable mixture, coating the rice in the lovely flavours. Then add the tin of chopped tomatoes and 800ml of the stock. Turn up the heat and bring everything to the boil.

5 Once the stock starts to boil, turn it down to a simmer and let the rice cook for 15 minutes, gently stirring to make sure that it doesn't stick.

6 Finally, add the peas and seafood to the pan, with a little more stock if the rice looks dry, and cook for a further 5 minutes.

7 Serve, sprinkled with parsley and lemon wedges.

Kedgeree

This is a delicious rice and smoked fish dish with a curry flavour. It works for breakfast, lunch or supper! It was popular in Victorian England after British travellers brought the recipe back from India.

Ingredients

2 eggs

500g smoked haddock, undyed if possible

150g basmati rice

Salt and pepper

100g butter

1 onion

1 garlic clove

2 teaspoons curry powder

1 lemon

1 small bunch flat leaf parsley

You will need a frying pan and two saucepans.

ALLERGIES

Dairy, eggs

NUMBER OF **4** SERVINGS

TIMINGS 30 MINUTES

You could also use coriander instead of parsley.

I think I have the same problem with coriander!

Method

1 Hard boil the eggs (see page 12 for instructions) and cook the rice (see page 110 for instructions). Check the fish for bones using your fingers.

You can use tweezers to remove any bones you find!

Fun Facts

Kedgeree originated from a concoction of spiced lentils, rice, fried onions and ginger known as *khichiri* dating back to the 14th century.

Florence Nightingale and Queen Victoria were especially partial to kedgeree.

2 Put the fish in the frying pan and cover with water. Bring to the boil, then simmer for 5 minutes until the fish is cooked. Remove from the pan and set aside.

3 Peel and chop the onions and garlic. Wipe out the frying pan, and melt the butter on a medium heat. Add the onions and garlic to the pan. Cook for 5 minutes without colouring, then add the curry powder. Cook for another 3 minutes.

4 Juice the lemon, break up the fish into large flakes and fluff up the rice with a fork. Add all three to the pan and stir carefully to coat in the curry mixture.

5 Peel the eggs and cut into quarters, and roughly chop the parsley. Add to the pan, gently mix and serve.

To make this even more delicious, you can add extra ingredients such as prawns or peas!

What about pineapple?

Pork Jambalaya

It's a very flexible dish as you can add anything you like.

Even ice cream?

Jambalaya comes from the French Quarter in New Orleans, USA, where Spanish settlers wanted to make paella, but had to substitute some of the ingredients.

Ingredients

1 onion
1 green pepper
3 celery stalks
200g pork loin
150g chorizo sausage
1 tablespoon olive oil
1 tablespoon smoked paprika

Salt and pepper
2 garlic cloves
2 tablespoons tomato purée
500ml chicken stock
400g tin of chopped tomatoes
200g long grain rice
180g frozen prawns, defrosted

You will need a large heavy-bottomed frying pan or casserole with a lid.

ALLERGIES

Shellfish

 NUMBER OF **6** SERVINGS

 TIMINGS **1 HOUR**

Method

1 Peel and chop the onion. Deseed and chop the pepper, and chop the celery stalks.

The combination of onion, pepper and celery is called the 'holy trinity' in Cajun cooking. Similar to the Italian soffritto or the French mirepoix.

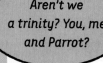

Aren't we a trinity? You, me and Parrot?

2 Chop the pork loin and chorizo into 2cm cubes. Add the oil to the pan on a medium heat, and add the pork and chorizo. Cook for 10 minutes until the pork is golden.

3 Add the chopped vegetables to the pan. Cook for 5 minutes until softened. Then add the paprika, and cook for 2 minutes.

4 Peel and finely chop the garlic cloves. Add to the pan with the tomato purée. Stir and cook for 1 minute.

5 Rinse the rice twice before adding to the pan with the chicken stock and tin of chopped tomatoes. Bring to the boil, before turning down to a very gentle simmer. Cover with a lid and cook for 20 minutes.

6 Check the rice is cooked, season with salt and pepper, add the prawns and cook for another 3–5 minutes. Serve immediately.

I'd be great on Bourbon Street, New Orleans!

KEY INGREDIENT
#6 Couscous

Tagine is the Moroccan name for both the stew and the cooking pot used to cook it in. Its distinctive shape means that all the cooking juices are kept in the meal.

I think it quite suits me!

Couscous is made from semolina, which is made from wheat flour, and is a staple in north African cuisines like Morocco and Tunisia. When cooked, couscous is light and fluffy, and the grains soak up a lot of flavour, so it is delicious with stews and tagines.

Moroccan Lamb Tagine

Ingredients

2 tablespoons olive oil
1 onion
2 carrots
500g diced leg of lamb
2 garlic cloves
1 teaspoon ground cumin
1 teaspoon ground ginger
2 teaspoons ground cinnamon

50g soft dried apricots
1 tablespoon honey
500ml chicken stock
500g butternut squash
240g couscous
1 small bunch flat leaf parsley
50g pine nuts (optional)

You will need a heavy-bottomed pan or casserole, 24cm in diameter.

ALLERGIES
Gluten, nuts, wheat

 NUMBER OF **6** SERVINGS

 TIMINGS 2 HOUR 30 MINUTES

How to cook couscous

To make the perfect couscous, you need to make sure you have the right amount of water to grains.

The general rule with couscous is that you need half as much water again as couscous. So, for every 100g of couscous, you need 150ml of boiling water.

Weigh your couscous (240g for this recipe) and put it in a bowl. Pour 360ml of boiling water over the couscous. Cover with a plate or tea towel and leave to soak for 15 minutes. When ready to serve, take a fork and fluff up the grains. Season with salt and pepper before serving.

Method

1 Finely dice the onion and carrots. Heat the oil in the pan on a medium heat and add the chopped vegetables. Cook for 5 minutes until soft.

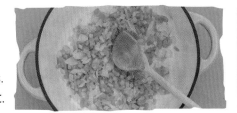

2 Add the diced lamb and fry until brown all over. Peel and chop the garlic. Add to the pan with the spices and cook for 3 minutes.

3 Chop the apricots into quarters. Add to the pan with the honey and stock. Stir to make sure the spices coat everything. Bring to the boil, then reduce to a simmer. Put on the lid, and cook for 1 hour.

4 Remove the lid and cook for 30 minutes. Peel the butternut squash. Cut in half and remove the seeds. Then chop into 2cm cubes. Add to the stew and cook for another 30 minutes.

5 Prepare the couscous. Chop the parsley. If using pine nuts, toast them over a medium heat in a dry frying pan for 1 minute.

6 Serve in bowls, and sprinkle with parsley and pine nuts.

I didn't know you could have fruit in a stew!

Mushroom Stroganoff

This dish replaces beef with mushrooms to make a delicious vegetarian version!

Stroganoff is a Russian dish traditionally made with beef and sour cream. It is named after Count Pavel Aleksandrovich Stroganoff, who loved French food, and asked for French mustard to be added to a Russian beef stew, along with some sour cream.

I think I would like to be Count Llama Allarma Llamaroff!

Ingredients

240g couscous
800g mushrooms
1 onion
1 tablespoon Dijon mustard
1 tablespoon English mustard
1 teaspoon smoked paprika
1 tablespoon Worcestershire sauce

300ml sour cream
30g butter
1 tablespoon olive oil
Salt and pepper
1 small bunch flat leaf parsley

You will need a frying pan.

ALLERGIES
Gluten, wheat

VEGETARIAN VEGETARIAN

NUMBER OF **4** SERVINGS

TIMINGS 25 MINUTES

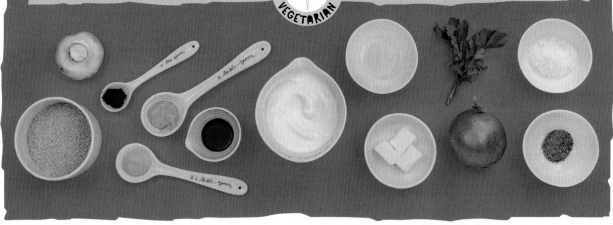

Method

1 Prepare the couscous (see page 73 for instructions).

2 Wipe the mushrooms clean, and chop into slices. Cut the onion in half and finely slice.

3 Mix the mustards, paprika, Worcestershire sauce and sour cream in a bowl.

4 Melt the butter in a frying pan over a medium heat and add the oil. Add the onion and cook for 5 minutes until softened. Add the mushrooms and cook until all their juices have evaporated, and the mushrooms are golden.

5 Add the sour cream mixture to the pan, mix and season with salt and pepper. Let the sauce simmer for 5 minutes.

Don't let the sauce boil too vigorously or it might split.

I don't believe in doing anything vigorously!

6 Fluff up the couscous and roughly chop the parsley.

7 Serve, sprinkling with parsley.

KEY INGREDIENT
#7 Chicken

Chicken is one of the most popular meats in the world. Used in every single country, there are hundreds of delicious dishes featuring this versatile bird!

I'm a versatile bird!

No you're not, you're a parrot!

Roast Chicken and All the Trimmings

There's nothing like a roast chicken dinner! The humble chicken is transformed through delicious gravy, tasty stuffing and pigs in blankets, plus amazing vegetables! (See pages 104–108 for the potatoes and vegetables.)

NUMBER OF **6** SERVINGS

TIMINGS **2 HOURS**

I'm not sure I want a blanket made of bacon!

Ingredients

For the stuffing
1 onion
4 streaky bacon rashers
1 small bunch parsley

200g sausage meat or minced pork
100g white breadcrumbs
Salt and pepper

ALLERGIES
Dairy, wheat

For the chicken

1 large whole chicken, weighing approx. 1.8kg

1 tablespoon olive oil

Salt and pepper

For the gravy

1 onion

15g butter

1 teaspoon olive oil

1 teaspoon soft brown sugar

1 tablespoon balsamic vinegar

1 teaspoon cornflour

300ml chicken stock

ALLERGIES

Dairy

For the pigs in blankets

1 pack of uncooked cocktail sausages (approx. 18)

9 streaky bacon rashers

You will need a roasting dish or tin for the chicken, two roasting trays and a saucepan.

Method

1 Heat the oven to 180°C / 400°F or gas mark 6. To make the stuffing, finely chop the onion. Using scissors, cut the bacon rashers into small pieces. Chop the parsley.

2 Put the sausage meat and breadcrumbs in a bowl with all the other ingredients, and mix.

Use your hands to squidge it all together!

4 To cook the stuffing with the chicken, use your fingers to loosen the chicken skin at the neck and push the stuffing gently into the space. If you prefer to cook the stuffing separately, form balls about 3cm in diameter, place on a roasting tray and cover with cling film. Put in the fridge until needed.

5 Put the chicken, with its stuffing, in a roasting dish. Rub the olive oil all over the chicken and season with salt and pepper. Place in the hot oven for 1 hour 45 minutes.

6 To make the gravy, finely slice the onion. Melt the butter in a pan and add the oil and onion. Cook for 8–10 minutes over a low heat until softened.

7 Add the sugar. This will caramelise (turn dark and sticky). Once the sugar has dissolved, add the balsamic vinegar and reduce until most of the liquid has disappeared.

8 Add the cornflour and stir. Let the mixture cook for 2 minutes, then add the chicken stock. Bring to the boil and then simmer for 20 minutes, stirring occasionally.

9 To make the pigs in blankets, Lay a bacon rasher on your chopping board and, using a knife, stretch it out. Cut the rasher in half, then use each half to wrap a cocktail sausage. Place on a roasting tray.

Pigs in blankets are mini sausages wrapped in bacon! They're really easy to make.

10 Half an hour before you want to eat, place the pigs in blankets (and stuffing balls if you're doing them) in the oven.

11 To finish the gravy, either strain through a sieve and press as much of the onion as you can back into the gravy using a metal spoon, or use a handheld blender to blitz the onion, to make a smooth gravy. Season with salt and pepper.

Ask a grown-up to help with this bit!

12 When the chicken has finished cooking, remove from the oven and leave to rest under kitchen foil for at least 15 minutes. It will stay hot for up to an hour if you need it to.

> To check if the chicken is cooked, you can use a meat thermometer, or take a sharp knife and insert it into the breast of the chicken. If the juices run clear, then it is cooked.

> Ask a grown-up to help here too!

13 Carve the chicken breasts into slices, and remove the meat from the chicken legs before serving with the pigs in blankets, stuffing and gravy.

> It smells like Christmas!

> Easy peasy, but don't forget to check it's cooked before taking out of the oven!

Of course, this is for a special occasion...

If you just want to roast a chicken, simply heat the oven to 180°C / 400°F or gas mark 6. Then rub it with oil and season, before cooking for 1 hour 45 minutes. Finally, let it rest for 15 minutes.

Creamy Chicken Curry

This chicken curry is based on an Indian dish called a korma. It is flavoured with spices including ground cumin and coriander, and has a sauce made from ground almonds and cream.

Some kormas use coconut milk instead of almonds, such as the vegetarian version on page 82.

I hear horses. Clippety clop, clip clop!

Ingredients

2 onions
1 thumb-sized piece of ginger
3 garlic cloves
45g butter
3 tablespoons vegetable oil
1 tablespoon ground coriander
1 tablespoon ground cumin
½ teaspoon ground turmeric
¼ teaspoon chilli powder
4 tablespoons ground almonds

1 tablespoon caster sugar
1½ teaspoons sea salt
4 chicken breasts
100ml double cream
Salt and pepper
300g basmati rice

You will need a large non-stick frying pan and a casserole.

ALLERGIES
Dairy, nuts

NUMBER OF
4
SERVINGS

TIMINGS
1 HOUR

Method

1 Peel and chop the onions. Peel and finely chop the garlic and ginger.

2 Melt the butter in the pan on a low heat. Add a tablespoon of oil to the pan, as well as the onions, ginger and garlic.

3 Cover and cook for 10 minutes. Then add the spices and stir, cooking for 5 minutes without the lid.

So that's the coriander, cumin, turmeric and chilli!

Shouldn't I know by now?

4 Add the almonds, sugar and salt, as well as 300ml of water to the pan, and gently simmer for 5 minutes, stirring regularly. Remove from the heat.

5 Cook the rice following the instructions on page 110.

6 Cut each chicken breast into eight bite-sized pieces. Season with salt and pepper. Heat the remaining oil in a frying pan, and fry the chicken pieces for 5 minutes, turning frequently until golden.

7 Using a stick blender or a food processor, blitz the onion mixture until smooth. Tip it into the pan with the chicken and simmer for 6 minutes, until the chicken is tender.

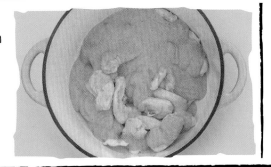

8 Add the cream and stir. Cook over a low heat for 2–3 minutes, stirring all the time.

9 Serve with rice or naan bread.

Creamy Vegetarian Curry

Most people in south India are vegetarian, so it's easy to find delicious vegetable curry recipes. Both curry recipes use the same spices.

If you like your curry spicy, double the amount of chilli and ginger in the recipe!

That's a bit too hot for me!

VEGETARIAN
VEGETARIAN

Ingredients

2 onions

1 thumb-sized piece of ginger

3 garlic cloves

45g butter

3 tablespoons vegetable oil

1 tablespoon ground coriander

1 tablespoon ground cumin

½ teaspoon ground turmeric

¼ teaspoon chilli powder

500g sweet potatoes

300ml vegetable stock

150ml coconut milk

400g tin of chopped tomatoes

1 teaspoon caster sugar

1 small cauliflower

1 broccoli head

300g basmati rice

You will need a heavy-bottomed pan or casserole, 28cm in diameter.

ALLERGIES

Dairy

NUMBER OF 4 SERVINGS

TIMINGS 45 MINUTES

Method

1 Follow steps 1–3 of the recipe for creamy chicken curry on the previous page.

2 Peel the sweet potatoes and chop into 2cm pieces. Add to the onion mixture and cook for 3 minutes, stirring regularly.

3 Cook the rice, following the instructions on page 110.

4 Stir in the stock, coconut milk, tomatoes and sugar. Bring the pan to the boil, and then simmer for 10 minutes.

5 Cut the cauliflower into small florets and add to the pan. Cook for 5 minutes.

6 Cut the broccoli into small pieces, then add to the pan. Cook for 5–10 minutes, uncovered, until the vegetables are cooked and the sauce has thickened.

You will need to stir the curry to make sure it doesn't stick to the pan!

Delicious!

7 Serve with rice or naan bread.

Barbecue Chicken and Pork Ribs

To marinate means to soak food in something seasoned before cooking. Often the acidity in the liquid helps to tenderise the meat.

Like this, you mean?

Barbecue sauce is a sticky, sweet and savoury sauce used to flavour meat or vegetables traditionally cooked on a barbecue. But you don't need to have an outdoor grill to enjoy the barbecue flavour, you can cook this recipe in the oven too. The trick is to marinate the meat in the sauce for as long as you can!

Ingredients

For the sauce:
4 spring onions
2 garlic cloves
1 thumb-sized piece of ginger
120ml tomato ketchup
30g dark brown soft sugar

1 tablespoon mustard
2 tablespoons Worcestershire sauce
4 tablespoons dark soy sauce
1 tablespoon vegetable oil

The meat:
8 chicken drumsticks
4 pork ribs

You will need two plastic bags and a roasting tin.

NUMBER OF 4 SERVINGS

TIMINGS 1 HOUR

NOT INCLUDING MARINATING TIME

Method

1 Roughly chop the spring onions. Peel and chop the garlic and ginger.

2 Place the onions, ginger and garlic in a food processor with all the other sauce ingredients, and blitz. Score the chicken and pork ribs with a sharp knife, two or three times each.

3 Tip half of the sauce into one plastic bag, and add the chicken drumsticks. Tip the remaining sauce into another plastic bag, and add the pork ribs. Place the chicken and ribs in the fridge to marinate for at least 2 hours, or up to 48 hours.

4 When you're ready to cook, heat the oven to 200°C / 425°F or gas mark 7. Once hot, tip the chicken and ribs into a roasting tin and cook for 40 minutes, basting occasionally with the sauce.

Basting means to spoon cooking juices over the meat, to keep it moist and add flavour!

Make sure you ask a grown-up to help!

Or you could use a turkey baster like this!

5 Serve with napkins!

Sweet and Sour Chicken

The sweet and sour sauce has pineapple and peppers to add sweetness and crunch!

This Chinese dish is a really popular takeaway classic. Try making it at home and serving with rice or noodles.

What's with all the fruit?

Ingredients

2 tablespoons vegetable oil
2 garlic cloves
1 thumb-sized piece of ginger
1 green pepper
1 red pepper
2 tablespoons tomato ketchup
4 tablespoons cider vinegar

1 teaspoon sesame oil
2 tablespoons light soy sauce
1 tablespoon soft brown sugar
430g can of pineapple chunks, drained
4 chicken breasts
300g long grain rice

You will need two saucepans and a non-stick frying pan.

NUMBER OF **4** SERVINGS

TIMINGS 30 MINUTES

Method

1 Cook the rice following the instructions on page 110.

2 Peel and finely chop the garlic cloves and ginger. Roughly chop both peppers and remove the seeds.

3 Heat the oil in a saucepan and add the garlic, ginger and peppers. Fry over a medium heat for 5 minutes.

4 Add the tomato ketchup, cider vinegar, sesame oil, soy sauce, sugar and pineapple to the pan. Bring to the boil and then simmer the sauce for 4 minutes until thickened.

5 Cut the chicken breasts into thin strips. Heat the oil in the frying pan on a medium heat, and add the chicken.

Depending on the size of your pan, you may need to do this in batches, otherwise the chicken won't turn golden.

6 Once the chicken is cooked, put it all back in the frying pan and add the sauce to warm through.

7 Serve in bowls.

Looks and smells absolutely delicious! Just like me!

Chicken Fajitas

This Mexican chicken dish can be spicy so it's great to make a batch of guacamole and tomato salsa to go alongside to cool things down.
See pages 31 and 32 for the recipes.

The recipe uses tortillas – you can make your own, or you can use ready-made ones instead!

Look at me!

That's how you make pizzas, not tortillas!

Ingredients

2 garlic cloves
1 lime, juiced
1 tablespoon smoked paprika
1 tablespoon ground coriander
1 teaspoon ground cumin
1 teaspoon ground cinnamon
½ teaspoon chilli powder
3 large chicken breasts

1 red onion
1 red pepper
1 green pepper
4 tablespoons olive oil
8 tortillas
300ml sour cream

You will need a plastic bag and a frying pan.

ALLERGIES
Dairy, gluten, wheat

NUMBER OF **4** SERVINGS

TIMINGS **30 MINUTES**

NOT INCLUDING MARINADING TIME

Method

1 To make the marinade, peel and crush the garlic. Put the crushed garlic in a plastic bag with the lime juice, smoked paprika, ground coriander, ground cinnamon and chilli powder.

2 Chop each chicken breast into strips 1cm wide – you should get eight or nine slices per breast. Add them to the plastic bag and leave to marinate for 1 hour.

3 Then chop the onion and peppers into thin slices. Fry over a high heat until slightly caramelised. Remove from the pan and keep warm.

4 When you're ready to cook the chicken, take it out of the fridge. Heat the oven to 160°C / 350°F or gas mark 4. Wrap the tortillas in foil and put in the oven to warm through.

5 Heat the frying pan on a high heat, tip the chicken and marinade into the pan and cook for 5–7 minutes. Turn regularly to keep the chicken from burning.

You may need to do this in batches if your pan isn't big enough!

Be careful though, as the pan will be hot.

6 Serve with tortillas, guacamole, salsa and sour cream on the side.

#8 Beef

Another very versatile ingredient, beef can be cooked as mince, roasted as a joint, fried as a steak or in a stir-fry, or slow-cooked in a casserole. Used in most cuisines around the world, it absorbs flavours really well too.

Beef Burgers

Burgers can be found in many fast-food restaurants, but it's very easy to make them yourself at home. You can add lots of different herbs or spices too.

Ingredients

½ small onion
1 egg yolk
500g beef mince
Salt and pepper
1 tablespoon vegetable oil

4 burger buns
1 small lettuce
Tomato salsa (optional) – see page 32
2 tablespoons mayonnaise (optional)
60g cheese (optional)

You will need a baking tray.

ALLERGIES

Dairy, eggs, gluten, wheat

NUMBER OF **4** SERVINGS

TIMINGS 1 HOUR 15 MINUTES

Method

1 Peel and finely chop the onion. Separate the egg yolk from the white (see page 110 for instructions). Place the yolk in a bowl with the mince and onion. Season with salt and pepper.

2 Mix together using a fork. Divide the mince into four and form into balls, about the size of a tennis ball.

It's easier if you wet your hands!

3 Flatten the balls into burgers, about 3cm thick, making sure that they are all the same size. Place on a baking tray, cover with cling film and put in the fridge to firm up for at least 45 minutes.

4 Heat the grill to high. Brush both sides of the burgers with vegetable oil. Grill for 8 minutes on each side until cooked. Remove from the grill and rest for 5 minutes.

If you're using cheese, add it to the top of the burgers for the last 2 minutes of cooking time.

5 Cut the burger buns in half and lightly toast under the grill. Put the burger on the bottom half of the bun. Layer lettuce, salsa and mayonnaise on top of the burger. Top with the other half of the bun and serve immediately.

Meatballs in Tomato and Pepper Sauce

Ingredients
2 small onions
1 egg yolk
400g beef mince
85g breadcrumbs
Salt and pepper

2 tablespoons olive oil
2 garlic cloves
400g tin of chopped tomatoes
450g jar of roasted peppers
3 tablespoons plain flour
Couscous, rice or flatbreads to serve

You will need a medium saucepan and a frying pan.

ALLERGIES
Eggs, gluten, wheat

NUMBER OF **4** SERVINGS

TIMINGS **1 HOUR**

Method

1 Peel and finely chop both onions, keeping one for the sauce. Separate the egg yolk from the white, and place the yolk with one of the chopped onions in a mixing bowl with the mince and breadcrumbs. Season with salt and pepper.

> It's best to use stale bread to make breadcrumbs. You can use a grater, but it's easier to use a food processor for this bit.

> I'm not a very good food processor.

2 Mix together and form into meatballs the size of ping-pong balls. Cover with cling film and put in the fridge for 30 minutes while you cook the sauce.

3 To make the sauce, heat 1 tablespoon of olive oil in a saucepan over a medium heat, and add the chopped onion. Cook gently for 5 minutes.

4 Peel and finely chop the garlic and add to the pan. Cook for 2 minutes before adding the chopped tomatoes. Drain the peppers and roughly chop, then add to the pan. Cook over a gentle heat for 15 minutes. Leave to cool and then blitz with a handheld blender or a liquidiser.

5 Heat the remaining oil in a frying pan. Place the plain flour on a plate and roll each meatball so it is coated with flour. Shake off any excess.

6 In batches, fry the meatballs, making sure to brown them all over. Cook for 15 minutes in total. Serve with rice, pasta, couscous or flatbreads and covered in sauce.

The Best Chilli Con Carne Ever!

Once you know how to make a chilli, you can make all sorts of Tex-Mex food including nachos, tacos and burritos!

Chilli comes from Mexico! In the 16th century, a Franciscan monk wrote about a chilli-pepper-spiced stew being eaten in Tenochtitlán, the Aztec capital, which is now the location of Mexico City. Its popularity spread north into Texas, USA, and now there is a cuisine called 'Tex-Mex' which is based on these flavours!

Tex-Mex, Tex-Mex!

Ingredients

500g pork mince
500g beef mince
1 tablespoon ground cinnamon
1 tablespoon smoked paprika
1 tablespoon ground cumin
1 tablespoon ground coriander
½ teaspoon ground chilli powder

2 large onions
2 garlic cloves
2 teaspoons soft brown sugar
300ml beef stock
400g tin of chopped tomatoes
400g tin of chickpeas
400g tin of red kidney beans
450g jar of roasted peppers
Salt and pepper

200g long grain rice
150ml sour cream

You will need
a large heavy-bottomed pan or casserole, 28cm in diameter.

ALLERGIES
Dairy

NUMBER OF 6 SERVINGS

TIMINGS 1 HOUR 15 MINUTES

You might think adding cinnamon to a savoury recipe seems odd, but it gives a real depth of flavour. Mexican recipes often add chocolate too!

I often add chocolate... to my mouth!

Method

1 Heat the pan over a high heat on the hob and add both minces. Cook for at least 10 minutes, stirring occasionally until the meat has caramelised.

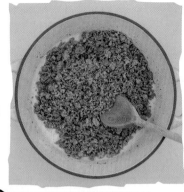

2 Add all the spices to the meat and let them cook out for 2–3 minutes. If you like spicy chilli, you can increase the amount of chilli powder!

If the pan is too hot, the spices might start to burn, so simply add a splash of water to cool the pan down.

3 Peel and chop the onions and garlic. Add them to the pan to absorb the spices for 5 minutes. Add the sugar and cook for another minute.

4 Add the stock and the chopped tomatoes. Drain the chickpeas and kidney beans and add to the pan.

5 Drain the peppers and roughly chop before adding to the pan. Bring to the boil and then turn down the heat to simmer, with the lid on, for at least 40 minutes. Stir occasionally to make sure the chilli isn't catching on the bottom.

6 Prepare the rice (see page 110 for instructions) and serve with sour cream on the side.

I think I put in too much chilli powder!

If the chilli is looking too runny, leave the pan lid half on, half off, so the steam can escape!

Fully-loaded Nachos

Nachos are a delicious snack to share with friends, and can be turned into a main meal with the addition of some leftover chilli!

Ingredients

200g leftover chilli

1 bag of tortilla chips

Salsa (see page 32 for recipe)

4 spring onions

200g grated cheese

Guacamole (see page 31 for recipe)

150ml sour cream

You will need a large baking tray.

Guacamole (see page 31 for recipe)

Salsa (see page 32 for recipe)

ALLERGIES

Dairy, gluten, wheat

NUMBER OF 4 SERVINGS

TIMINGS 15 MINUTES

Method

1 Heat the grill on high and warm up the leftover chilli in a pan or in the microwave.

2 Spread the tortilla chips out on a baking tray. Dollop the chilli and salsa over the tortilla chips. Do the same with the grated cheese.

3 Place under the grill for 3–5 minutes until the cheese melts.

4 Slice the spring onions and sprinkle over the top. Serve with the guacamole and sour cream!

Be careful with the grill. The baking tray will be very hot.

Beef Steak Sandwich

There are lots of different types of steak and each one has a different characteristic depending on which part of the cow it comes from!

We use different types of steaks for different recipes!

Types of steak

Fillet – the most tender and mild-flavoured steak.

Sirloin – slightly more texture and a beefier flavour.

Rump – lots of flavour but less tender than sirloin.

Ribeye – lots of fat marbling through the meat to give a great flavour.

T-bone – includes the bone and has two steaks for the price of one.

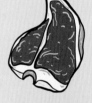

Flank – lean and best cut into thin strips.

Ingredients

2 garlic cloves

4 thyme sprigs

1 tablespoon red wine vinegar

3 tablespoons olive oil

2 sirloin steaks, 200g each

2 red onions

30g butter

1 French baguette

2 teaspoons mustard (optional)

You will need two non-stick frying pans and a plastic bag.

ALLERGIES

Dairy, gluten, wheat

NUMBER OF **2** SERVINGS

TIMINGS **40 MINUTES**

NOT INCLUDING MARINADING TIME

How do you like your steak cooked?

Rare – warm but not cooked in the centre, lightly charred on the outside and soft to the touch.

Medium rare – the steak centre is pink, the sides browned, and the top and bottom caramelised. It should spring back to the touch.

Medium – more brown than pink in the centre, and feels firm to the touch.

Medium well – only a very small hint of pink in the middle, and feels very stiff to the touch.

Well done – no pink in the middle, but shouldn't be burnt on the outside either. It feels solid to the touch.

I like my steak done every way!

Method

1 Peel and finely chop the garlic cloves. Strip the thyme sprigs and put the leaves and garlic into a plastic bag. Add the red wine vinegar, a tablespoon of olive oil and the steaks to the bag and seal. Marinate in the fridge for at least an hour.

The marinade adds flavour and tenderises the steak!

I use hooves to tenderise my steak!

You can't just trample it, silly!

2 Peel and slice the onions. Heat the butter and a tablespoon of olive oil in a frying pan. Once sizzling, add the onions and cook over a medium heat for 20 minutes until dark and sticky. Stir occasionally.

3 When ready to cook the steaks, remove them from the fridge so they reach room temperature. Take out of the bag and pat dry, making sure you take the garlic and thyme off the steak before cooking.

Otherwise they will burn and taste bitter!

4 Heat a frying pan on a medium high heat. Brush the steaks with olive oil on both sides, and add to the pan. Cook for 1 minute, then turn them using kitchen tongs. For medium rare, turn each steak every minute, for 7 minutes. Subtract a minute for rare, or add a minute for medium.

The caramelisation is called the 'Maillard reaction'. By turning the steaks regularly, you encourage the flavour on the outside, while making sure the insides stay tender.

5 Once cooked to perfection, remove the pan from the heat and let the steaks rest for 5 minutes. This keeps the juices in the steak. If you cut into it immediately, all the juicy goodness drains away.

6 Cut the French baguette in half lengthways. If using mustard, spread a thin layer on one half. Top with the caramelised onions. Cut the steaks into slices 1cm thick and place on top of the onions. Drizzle any juices in the pan on to the top layer of baguette. Cut into two sandwiches and serve.

KEY INGREDIENT
#9 Fish

Ooh good! I could use a brain boost!

Fish is really good for your health and helps to keep your brain working well! It's also quick to cook, so is great for times when you need food fast! Check out some more fish recipes on pages 28 and 68.

Quick Fish Lunches

Horseradish belongs to the same family as mustard, which explains its hot taste!

Be careful not to get any in your eyes!

Mackerel Paté

Ingredients

1 lemon
125g full fat cream cheese
2 teaspoons horseradish
Salt and pepper
140g smoked mackerel fillets
Buttered toast to serve

ALLERGIES

Dairy, gluten, wheat

NUMBER OF **4** SERVINGS

TIMINGS **5 MINUTES**

Method

1 Zest and juice the lemon.

2 Put the cream cheese, horseradish, lemon zest and juice, and salt and pepper, in a bowl and mix.

3 Remove the skin from the mackerel fillets and flake into the cream cheese mixture. Mix gently.

4 Serve with hot buttered toast!

That's not how you serve toast!

Smoked Salmon Open Sandwiches

> A gherkin is a pickled cucumber!

> I think I'm in a bit of a pickle myself!

Ingredients

2 soft-boiled eggs
4 slices of rye bread
100g smoked salmon
4 cocktail gherkins
2 tablespoons crème fraiche

ALLERGIES
Dairy, gluten, wheat

NUMBER OF SERVINGS **4**

TIMINGS **15 MINUTES**

Method

1 Cook the eggs until soft-boiled (see page 12 for instructions). Once cool, remove the shell and slice into six pieces.

2 Lay the smoked salmon on the bread. Add the egg slices. Slice the gherkins, and arrange on top of the egg and salmon.

3 Put the crème fraiche in a bowl and stir to loosen, then drizzle over the top!

Prawn Cocktail

Ingredients

1 iceberg or little gem lettuce
150g cooked king prawns
2 tablespoons mayonnaise
2 teaspoons tomato ketchup

½ lemon, juiced
Salt and pepper
¼ teaspoon smoked paprika (optional)

ALLERGIES
Eggs, shellfish

NUMBER OF SERVINGS **4**

TIMINGS **10 MINUTES**

> Don't think much of this cocktail!

Method

1 Chop the lettuce and divide into four bowls. Share the prawns equally between the bowls.

2 Mix the mayonnaise, tomato ketchup and lemon juice in a bowl, then season with salt and pepper. Spoon over the prawns. If using, sprinkle a little paprika on top, then serve.

Three delicious fish lunches!

Baked Salmon with Miso Dressing

Miso is a thick paste made from soya beans and comes from Japan.

These salmon fillets are baked in the oven in foil parcels, which cook the fish and the vegetables in a lovely miso dressing at the same time.

Ingredients

1 thumb-sized piece of ginger
2 tablespoons miso paste (red or white)
2 tablespoons runny honey
2 tablespoons rice wine vinegar
4 tablespoons light soy sauce
2 teaspoons sesame oil

2 heads of pak choi
2 carrots
8 spring onions
4 salmon fillets

You will need a baking tray and some kitchen foil.

Pak choi, or bok choi, is a type of Chinese cabbage.

Pak choi, bok choi, I can chop choi!

NUMBER OF **4** SERVINGS

TIMINGS **30 MINUTES**

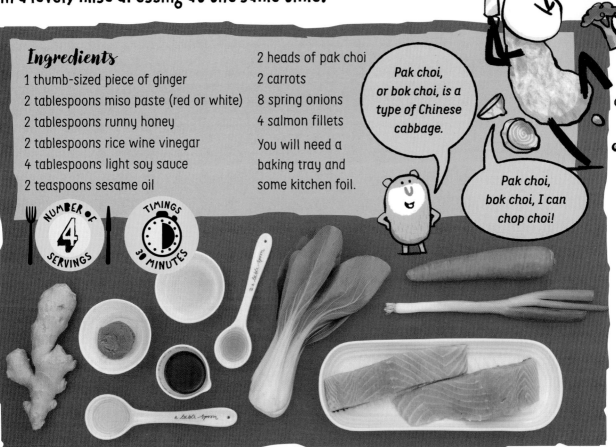

Method

1 Heat the oven to 160°C / 350°F or gas mark 4.

2 Peel and grate the ginger. In a bowl, mix the ginger with the miso, honey, vinegar, soy sauce and sesame oil.

100

3 Chop each head of pak choi in half lengthways, so you have four pieces. Peel the carrots and slice into long strips. Slice the spring onions.

4 If the salmon has any skin, remove it by placing the salmon skin-side down on a board, short edge towards you. Take a knife and, holding the short edge, slide the knife between the skin and the fish, along the board.

Always make sure the knife is pushing away from you!

5 Tear four pieces of kitchen foil, 35cm x 25cm, and place on the baking tray. Divide the vegetables into the middle of the foil sheets and place a salmon fillet on top.

6 Bring the foil up around the vegetables and salmon, and then close up at each end, leaving the fish visible. Share the miso sauce between the parcels, drizzling to cover all the fish and vegetables. Bake in the oven for 15 minutes.

7 Remove from the oven and serve with noodles or rice.

Fish Pie

This dish is wonderfully comforting, with tasty fish and a creamy mashed potato topping. You can use whatever fish you like, but the pie is especially delicious if you include smoked fish like smoked haddock or smoked cod.

Ingredients

800g potatoes
3 eggs
250g frozen whole leaf spinach, or fresh
1 onion
1 carrot
30g butter

300ml double cream
75g Parmesan
1 lemon, juiced
500g fish (salmon, cod, smoked haddock etc.)
150g raw king prawns (optional)
Salt and pepper

You will need a frying pan, a large saucepan and an ovenproof dish, 23cm x 28cm.

ALLERGIES

Eggs, dairy, shellfish

NUMBER OF **6** SERVINGS

TIMINGS **1 HOUR**

Make sure you use potatoes that are good for mashing, such as Maris Piper!

I can see that this is going to get messy!

Method

1 Peel the potatoes and cut into chunks. Place in a large pan and cover with boiling water. Add a pinch of salt and cook for 10 minutes.

2 Add the eggs to the potato pan and cook for another 10 minutes. When the time is up, fish out the eggs using a slotted spoon and leave to cool. Drain the potatoes in a colander and return to the pan.

3 Defrost the frozen spinach and squeeze out any excess water. If using fresh, cook in a frying pan with a knob of butter until all the moisture has gone.

4 Peel and chop the onion and carrot into small pieces. Melt 15g of butter in a frying pan, and gently cook the onion and carrot for 5 minutes.

5 Add almost all the cream and bring to nearly a boil. Remove from the heat and add the Parmesan and lemon juice.

6 Mash the potatoes with butter and the little cream you have left (see page 105 for instructions). Peel and quarter the eggs.

7 Heat the oven to 180°C / 400°F or gas mark 6. To make the pie, chop the fish into bite-size pieces and add it to the pie dish, with the prawns if using. Spread the spinach over the fish, add the egg quarters and cover with the cream sauce. Carefully spoon the mashed potato over the top.

You could use a palette knife to spread the potato on top of the filling. If you go around the edges of the dish before filling in the middle, then the sauce won't escape!

8 Bake in the oven for 30 minutes. Remove and serve with peas or beans.

My sauce is definitely escaping!

CORE SKILL
#5 Vegetable Sides

VEGETARIAN VEGETARIAN

Most of the dishes in the book have their own vegetables as part of the recipe, but there will be times when you need something extra to add to the main event. Here are eight side dishes that you can add to almost any dish!

Roast Potatoes

Crunchy on the outside, soft and fluffy on the inside, roast potatoes finish off a roast chicken dinner beautifully.

Ingredients
800g Maris Piper potatoes
50ml olive oil
2 tablespoons semolina
Salt and pepper

You will need a roasting tin.

ALLERGIES
Wheat, gluten

NUMBER OF **6** SERVINGS

TIMINGS 1 HOUR

Method

1 Heat the oven to 200°C / 425°F or gas mark 7.

2 Peel the potatoes. Cut into even-sized chunks 3–4cm in size. Cook in a pan of boiling water for 5 minutes, then drain through a colander.

3 While the potatoes are cooking, pour the olive oil into the roasting tin and put in the oven.

4 Tip the potatoes back in the pan, add the semolina. Put the lid on the pan and, holding tightly, give the pan a good shake.

5 Carefully take the roasting tin out of the oven and tip the potatoes into the oil.

Ask a grown-up to help if the pan is too heavy.

This makes the outsides nice and rough, so the potatoes can soak up the oil.

Be careful, as the oil can splash.

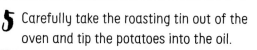

6 Using rubber tongs, carefully turn each potato so it is covered in the oil. Season with salt and pepper. Put back in the oven and cook for at least 40 minutes until all golden and brown. Turn the potatoes twice during the cooking process.

Mashed Potatoes

Creamy smooth mashed potatoes are delicious on top of a fish pie!

Ingredients
800g potatoes

30g butter

1 tablespoon milk or cream

Salt and pepper

You will need a large saucepan.

ALLERGIES
Dairy

NUMBER OF **6** SERVINGS

TIMINGS 30 MINUTES

Method

1 Peel the potatoes and cut into similar sized chunks.

So they cook evenly!

2 Put in a pan and pour boiling water over to cover. Bring to the boil and then simmer for 15–20 minutes, until a knife cuts through them easily.

3 Drain the potatoes through a colander and return to the pan. Add the butter and cream or milk, and mash until smooth. Then season.

Courgette and Polenta Chips

Parmesan crusted vegetable chips made with polenta! Absolutely delicious with a burger!

Ingredients
15g butter

1 tablespoon olive oil

2 courgettes

1 garlic clove

125g instant polenta

75g Parmesan

You will need a rectangular dish and a baking tray.

ALLERGIES
Dairy

Substitute the Parmesan cheese with a vegetarian hard cheese to make this vegetarian.

NUMBER OF **4** SERVINGS · TIMINGS 1 HOUR 30 MINUTES

Method

1 Melt the butter with the oil in a frying pan.

2 Grate the courgette on the large side of the grater and add to the frying pan. Peel and chop the garlic and add to the courgette. Fry for 15 minutes, until soft and golden.

3 Grate the Parmesan. Put 500ml of water into a pan and bring to the boil. Add the polenta and cook for 5 minutes, stirring all the time.

Be careful, as the polenta can bubble and spit!

Is it angry?

It spits almost as well as I do!

4 Add the courgette and 50g of Parmesan to the polenta, and cook for another 2 minutes.

5 Lightly grease a rectangular dish, 20cm x 25cm, with olive oil and tip the polenta mixture into the dish. Leave to cool slightly before putting in the fridge for 30 minutes.

6 Heat the oven to 200°C / 425°F or gas mark 7. Oil a baking tray. Take the polenta out of the fridge and cut into chips. Toss with the remaining 25g of Parmesan and place on the baking tray.

7 Cook for 30 minutes, turning once.

Sweet Potato Fries

Super easy! Simply peel, chop into fries, toss in a little oil and seasoning in a roasting tin, and bake in the oven for 30 minutes.

Even I can do these!

Roasted Carrots

Ingredients

1kg carrots
2 tablespoons olive oil
2 tablespoons honey

1 tablespoon cider vinegar
Salt and pepper

You will need a roasting tin.

NUMBER OF **6** SERVINGS

TIMINGS 45 MINUTES

Method

1 Heat the oven to 180°C / 400°F or gas mark 6. Peel the carrots and cut in half lengthways.

Or quarters if they're really large!

2 Toss in a large roasting tin with the olive oil, honey and cider vinegar. Season and roast for 40 minutes.

Sesame Broccoli

Ingredients

1 large head of broccoli
1 garlic clove
½ thumb-sized piece of ginger
1 tablespoon sesame oil
2 tablespoons sesame seeds

You will need a frying pan with a lid.

I love little trees!

NUMBER OF **4** SERVINGS

TIMINGS 15 MINUTES

Method

1 Separate the broccoli into florets. Peel and finely chop the garlic and ginger.

2 Heat the oil in a frying pan on a medium heat. Add the garlic and ginger and cook for 1 minute before adding the broccoli. Add 2 tablespoons of water and cook with the lid on for 5 minutes.

3 Remove the lid and cook until the water has disappeared. Finally add the sesame seeds to the pan and toss around. Season.

Braised Red Cabbage

Ingredients

1 small red cabbage
1 red onion
70g soft brown sugar
70ml cider vinegar

30g butter
Salt and pepper

You will need a large heavy-bottomed pan or casserole, 28cm in diameter.

TIMINGS
1 HOUR 45 MINUTES

ALLERGIES
Dairy

The red cabbage can turn a wooden spoon purple, so use a plastic one instead.

Method

1 Chop the cabbage into quarters and remove the white core. Finely shred. Peel and finely slice the red onion.

2 Heat the pan and add the cabbage, onion, sugar, vinegar, butter and 150ml of water. Season well. Stir to mix. Bring to the boil and then simmer. Cover with a lid and cook on a low heat for at least an hour, stirring occasionally.

3 Remove the lid and cook for a further 30 minutes until the cabbage is cooked.

Too late!

Stir-fried Garlic Green Beans

Ingredients

200g green beans
2 tablespoons vegetable oil

2 garlic cloves
1 tablespoon dark soy sauce

You will need a wok.

NUMBER OF
4
SERVINGS

TIMINGS
10 MINUTES

Method

1 Trim the ends of the green beans. Peel and finely slice the garlic cloves.

2 Heat the oil in a wok. Stir-fry the beans for 4 minutes until they are almost cooked through.

3 Add the garlic and cook for another minute before adding the soy sauce. Stir-fry for another minute.

Cooking Techniques

Knives and chopping

Always use a chopping board to protect your work surface, and to make it easier to move your ingredients from the work surface to the pan. Make sure your chopping board is sturdy and won't slide around by placing it on a tea towel. Some have rubber feet that help them stay in place.

There are lots of different kitchen knives designed to do specific tasks, such as filleting a fish or boning a chicken. For the recipes in this book, you need three basic knives.

Different knives do different jobs in a kitchen.

There are over 19 different ways to chop vegetables! We only need to worry about three!

small paring knife

utility knife

bread knife

1 **Chop.** This is to cut into irregular pieces, but normally of similar size.

2 **Dice.** This means to cut into even-sized cubes, like dice. They can be small, medium or large dice.

3 **Slice.** This is straightforward and means even-width cuts, like slicing an onion.

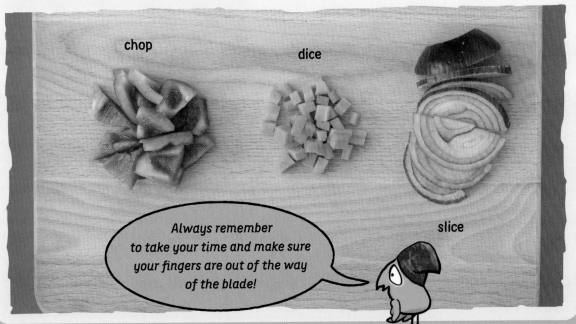

chop

dice

slice

Always remember to take your time and make sure your fingers are out of the way of the blade!

Separating eggs

It's important to remember to go slowly and carefully. If even a tiny bit of yolk gets into the egg whites, they won't whisk properly.

> Once you've learnt how to separate an egg into its white (the clear liquid bit) and its yolk (the yellow circle), there are all sorts of recipes you can make.

1 Getting your hands dirty

> With clean hands, obviously!

Over a bowl, crack the egg on the side of the bowl or with a knife. Use your hand to scoop up the egg, and let the egg white dribble through.

2 Using a slotted spoon

Place the spoon in a bowl. Crack the egg into it. Let the white run through and off the spoon and lift the yolk clear.

> It's no yolk, I'm not very good at this.

How to cook the perfect rice

> Perfect for the kedgeree on page 68.

The secret to cooking rice, so that the grains fluff up and don't stick together, is to make sure you wash the rice at least three times so that most of the starch has been rinsed away.

1 Weigh out your rice, 75g per person, and place in a saucepan. Fill with water, swirl around for a few seconds, then drain through a sieve. Repeat twice.

2 To cook the rice, cover with cold water until there is 2.5cm over the level of the rice.

3 Boil the rice for 5 minutes, uncovered, until most of the liquid has evaporated and you can see little craters in the surface.

4 Turn the heat right down, cover the pan with a lid and cook for at least 20 minutes without stirring.

5 Finally, rest the rice for 5 minutes before serving.

Garlic and ginger

The recipes use a lot of garlic and ginger, so here's how to peel and chop them!

Garlic

1 Remove a clove from the bulb.

2 Using the small paring knife, chop off the bottom end and remove the purple skin.

3 Finely chop the garlic into tiny pieces.

4 If the recipe asks for crushed garlic and you don't have a garlic crusher, use the blade of the knife and draw it over the garlic, pressing down to squeeze the pieces.

sliced   finely   crushed
          chopped

Ginger

1 Using a vegetable peeler, remove the brown skin of the ginger.

2 Then you can either grate or finely slice and then dice the ginger.

sliced

finely chopped

grated

Acknowledgements

With thanks to Mr Griff, illustrator extraordinaire; Tina, the wondrous photographer; Karen, the amazing chef's assistant; the various Noodle Juice family members who put up with the ceaseless cooking and photo shoots, and last, but not least, the frying pan!

(Only washed approximately 250 times in two weeks!)

I CAN COOK

Index

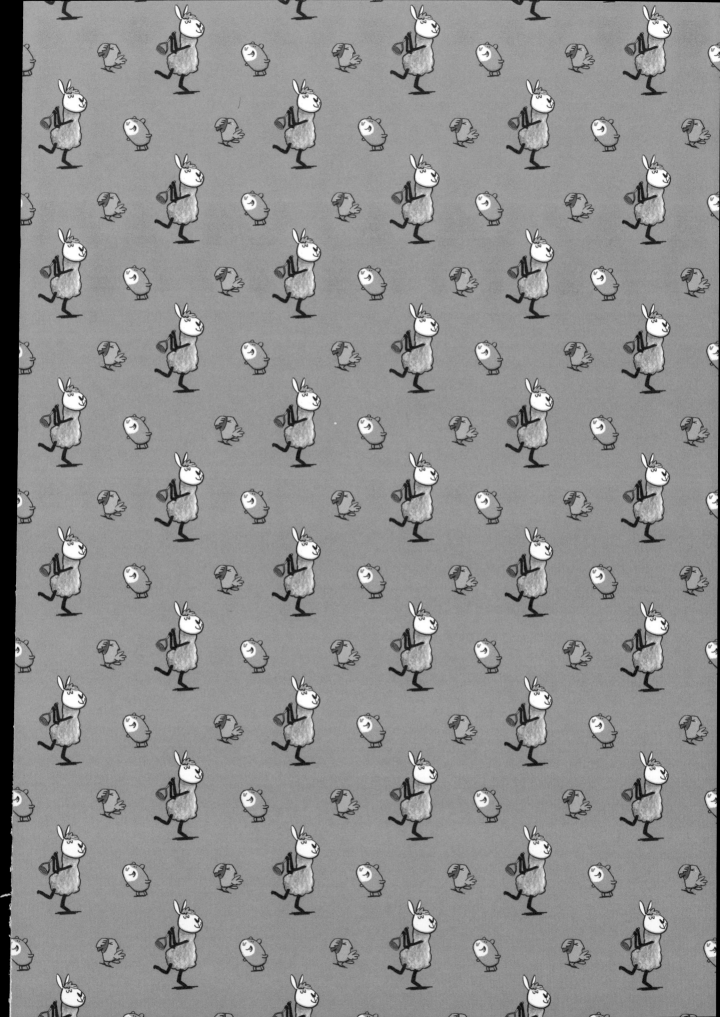

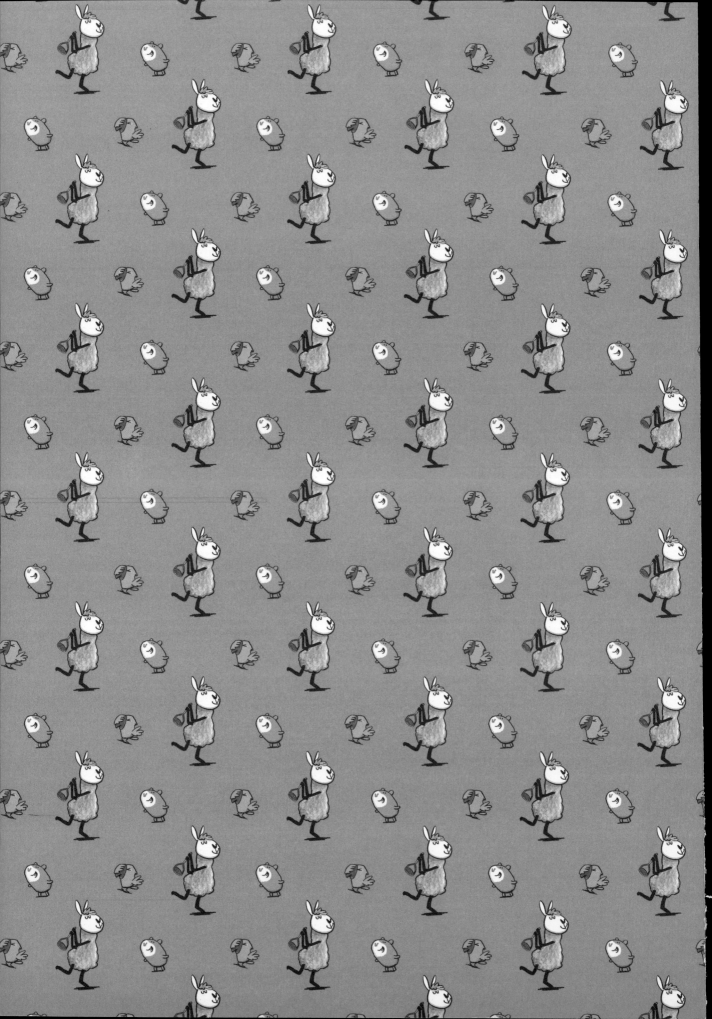